AI Consultant Core Knowledge and Skills

By

Othman Omran Khalifa

2024

Copyright

Acknowledgment

This book, *AI Consultant: Core Knowledge and Skills*, is the culmination of a shared passion for the transformative potential of artificial intelligence and the desire to empower consultants to harness this power effectively. I am deeply grateful to all those who have supported me throughout this journey.

I extend my heartfelt gratitude to my family for their unwavering encouragement and belief in my vision. Their support has been a constant source of strength and motivation.

I am immensely grateful to the readers of this book. Your interest in mastering AI consulting is a testament to your commitment to innovation and progress. It is my hope that this book equips you with the tools and knowledge needed to make a lasting impact in your consulting career and the world of AI.

Thank you all for being a part of this journey.

Sincerely.

Othman Omran Khalifa

Preface

Artificial intelligence (AI) has transformed sectors throughout the world, changing the way firms operate, develop, and expand. AI's effect is evident in fields such as healthcare, finance, education, manufacturing, etc. However, maximizing AI's potential takes more than just technical competence; it also involves strategic vision, an awareness of business needs, and the ability to convert complicated AI concepts into effective solutions. This is when AI consultancy becomes critical.

This book is intended to serve as a thorough reference for individuals hoping to work as AI consultants, as well as seasoned professionals looking to improve their abilities. It attempts to bridge the gap between AI theory and practical application, providing readers with the skills and information they need to thrive in this dynamic and fast changing subject.

The book consists of Nine chapters; Chapter One presents the foundations of AI consulting and outlines its significance and reach, marks the start of the trip. The fundamental ideas and technology that support AI systems are covered in Chapter Two, which explains the essential AI knowledge that every consultant needs to possess. To match AI capabilities with organizational objectives, readers will need to be able to recognize AI potential for organizations, which is covered in Chapter 3. Chapter Four focuses on creating a successful AI strategy, which walks readers through the process of customizing AI solutions to fit particular customer requirements. The importance of data in AI is emphasized in Chapter 5, which also offers advice on efficient data management and preparation methods. Chapter Six goes into great depth about creating and implementing AI models, which are the technical foundation of AI consulting.

Chapter Seven examines the platforms and technologies that make AI development and implementation easier if they want to be successful in this field. Also, provides helpful guidance on how to choose and utilize them. In Chapter Eight, the emphasis switches to the human element of consulting, including methods for establishing trusting connections with clients and producing solutions that provide value. Chapter Nine concludes by discussing the business side of AI consulting and providing advice on how to promote services and scale operations for sustainability and long-term success.

This book strikes a mix between strategic insight and technical depth, and it is enhanced by real-world examples and useful advice. This book will enable readers to unleash AI's transformational potential for businesses and organizations, regardless of their background—whether they are a business professional investigating AI application, an aspiring AI consultant, or a tech enthusiast looking to expand your knowledge.

Author

Othman Omran Khalifa

Contents

Chapter One
Introduction to AI Consulting

1.1.Overview of AI consulting and its growing demand in the industry

AI consulting has grown significantly in our daily lives, particularly inside industries. It is driven by the growing use of artificial intelligence in a variety of sectors. Businesses are hiring AI consultants to assist them negotiate the challenges of incorporating AI technology into their operations, increase productivity, and gain a competitive advantage. AI consultants provide professional advice on how to use machine learning, data analysis, and automation technologies, which are essential for improving business processes and decision-making. Retailers, for example, are utilizing AI to improve supply chains, forecast client preferences, and customize shopping experiences, all of which require specific knowledge to properly apply.

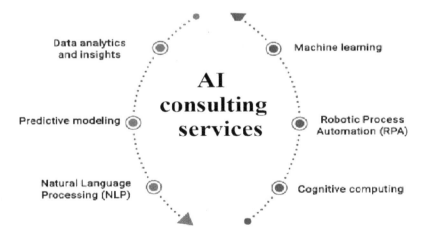

Figure 1.1. AI Consulting Services

The increased demand for AI consulting services stems from a requirement for knowledge in fast emerging AI technology. Figure 1.1 shows how to become AI consultant. Many businesses, particularly small and medium-sized corporations, lack the in-house skills and resources to fully realize AI's promise. AI consultants assist bridge this gap by offering customized solutions like predictive analytics models, robotic process automation (RPA), and natural language processing (NLP) technologies, which allow businesses to automate mundane operations and make data-driven choices. For example, in the financial services industry, AI consultants assist banks in deploying AI-powered fraud detection systems that can spot suspicious transactions in real time, lowering risks and operating costs.

Another factor contributing to the expansion of AI consulting is the advent of cloud-based AI platforms, which have made AI more accessible to organizations of all sizes. Consultants play an important role in helping firms incorporate these platforms into their existing IT architecture. For example, in healthcare, AI consultants help hospitals implement AI systems that can evaluate medical pictures, forecast patient outcomes, and aid with diagnoses. These advances not only enhance patient care, but also simplify hospital operations, resulting in cost savings.

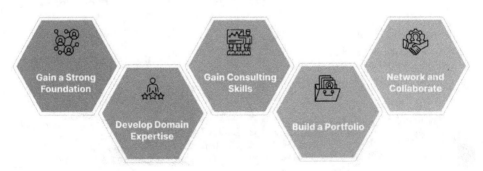

Figure 1.2. How to Become an AL Consultant

As AI transforms industries such as manufacturing, healthcare, finance, and retail, the need for specialist AI consulting services is likely to rise. As AI technologies like deep learning and computer vision progress, businesses will increasingly rely on consultants to help them remain ahead of the competition, adapt to shifting market dynamics, and capitalize on the immense potential of AI-driven breakthroughs.

1.2.Roles and responsibilities of an AI consultant

An AI consultant is responsible for advising enterprises through the adoption and integration of artificial intelligence technology into their operations. Their tasks include analyzing a company's needs and delivering bespoke AI solutions that are aligned with the company's goals. One of an AI consultant's key responsibilities is to assess the organization's present technology infrastructure and suggest areas where AI might enhance efficiency, save costs, or offer new possibilities. For example, an AI consultant working with a manufacturing organization may find how machine learning algorithms might be used to optimize production processes, minimize downtime, and enhance quality control by detecting equipment breakdowns ahead of time.

Another important role of an AI consultant is to create specialized AI strategies. Consultants collaborate extensively with stakeholders to understand their unique business objectives before developing a roadmap for AI adoption that includes the selection of relevant technology and solutions. In the retail business, for example, an AI consultant may assist a firm in developing a customer-centric AI strategy by advising the installation of AI-driven recommendation systems that utilize consumer data to tailor product choices, resulting in increased sales and satisfaction.

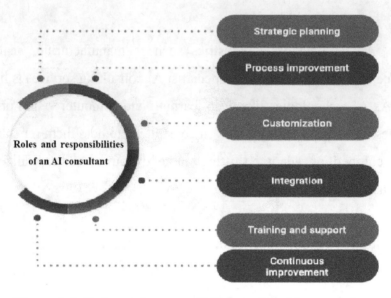

Figure 1.3. Roles and responsibilities of an AI consultant

AI consultants are also in charge of managing the implementation of AI solutions, ensuring that these technologies fit seamlessly into current workflows without causing interruptions. Before deploying AI models, IT teams and data scientists must collaborate to create and evaluate them. In the healthcare industry, for example, AI consultants have assisted hospitals in implementing AI systems for analyzing patient data to predict health outcomes and optimize treatment methods. Consultants verify that these systems are dependable, consistent with standards, and secure, particularly when dealing with sensitive patient data.

Aside from technical competence, AI consultants work on staff training and creating an AI-friendly culture within the firm. They provide education and training programs to help staff understand how to use AI products efficiently. For example, an AI consultant working with a financial services organization may provide seminars for employees on how to understand the results of AI-based fraud detection systems, allowing them to make educated decisions based on AI-generated insights. This assures that the organization can fully utilize AI capabilities while still requiring human control.

However, ongoing monitoring and improvement are among an AI consultant's long-term obligations. After the first deployment, AI consultants frequently work with the organization to evaluate performance, fine-tune algorithms, and modify AI systems as the business grows. In the case of a logistics company, for example, an AI consultant may conduct periodic reviews of the effectiveness of AI-powered route optimization software to verify that cost savings continue to be delivered when delivery patterns and business demands change. The following are the summary and key roles and responsibilities:

1.*Assessment and Analysis*: AI experts examine an organization's present technology capabilities and suggest areas where AI might provide value. This includes evaluating data, understanding corporate processes, and identifying areas where AI may improve efficiency or drive innovation.

2. *Strategic Planning*: After doing an evaluation, AI consultants create a bespoke plan that aligns with the organization's objectives. They provide a road map for adopting AI solutions, from selecting relevant technology to setting goals and KPIs (key performance indicators).

3. *AI Solution Design*: Consultants create customized AI solutions to meet unique corporate goals. This may include suggesting machine learning models, natural language processing (NLP) systems, or predictive analytics tools, and ensuring that these solutions align with the company's goals and capabilities.

4. *Implementation and Integration*: An AI consultant's primary responsibility is to manage the implementation of AI technologies. This involves integrating AI technologies into current IT infrastructure to ensure

they work seamlessly with other applications and systems without creating disturbance.

5. *Data Management and Preparation*: AI experts help organize and prepare clean, organized data for AI applications. This frequently includes data purification, tagging, and the creation of data pipelines to facilitate model training and implementation.

6. *Model Training and Testing*: These steps involve training AI models using corporate data and validating their performance through testing. This guarantees that the AI solutions are accurate, dependable, and satisfy the performance requirements before they are completely implemented.

7. *Training and Change Management*: AI consultants teach workers and stakeholders how to utilize AI products successfully. They also help to create an AI-friendly culture within the firm by raising awareness and preparing teams for AI adoption.

8. *Continuous Monitoring and Optimization*: After implementation, AI experts continue to monitor the functioning of the systems. They fine-tune algorithms, fix any issues, and alter models when company requirements or market conditions change.

9. *Compliance and Ethical AI Use*: AI consultants verify AI solutions adhere to industry norms and ethical standards, especially when dealing with sensitive data. This is especially important in industries like as healthcare, banking, and retail, where data privacy and compliance are paramount.

10. *Support for Innovation and Scalability*: As the organization expands, AI consultants help scale AI solutions to accommodate more datasets, higher complexity, and more users. They also look at new AI advancements that might boost the company's competitive edge.

Overall, AI consultants play an important role in helping firms use AI technology to increase operational efficiency, generate innovation, and accomplish strategic objectives.

1.3. Skills Needed for Aspiring AI Consultants

Aspiring AI consultants need a varied set of talents that include technical competence, commercial acumen, and communication ability. These talents enable them to traverse difficult AI projects, provide actionable insights, and assist organizations in realizing the full potential of artificial intelligence.

1. ***Strong Technical Proficiency in AI and Machine Learning***: An AI consultant must have a thorough grasp of AI technologies including ML, deep learning, NLP, and computer vision. This expertise enables consultants to create and apply AI models that are suited to specific business situations. For example, an AI consultant working with a retail organization may create a recommendation engine that uses machine learning algorithms to assess client behavior and personalize product recommendations. Building and fine-tuning models requires proficiency in programming languages like as Python and R, as well as frameworks such as TensorFlow or PyTorch.

2. ***Data Analysis and Management***: Consultants with good data analysis abilities can efficiently manage massive datasets, which are important to AI. AI consultants must understand how to clean, filter, and analyze data in order to identify patterns and insights. They must also grasp how to work with both organized and unstructured data. For example, an AI consultant working with a healthcare provider may need to assess patient data from several sources, such as electronic health records and medical imaging, in order to develop predictive models for patient diagnosis.

Understanding SQL, data pipelines, and big data solutions such as Hadoop or Spark is essential for handling and processing massive datasets.

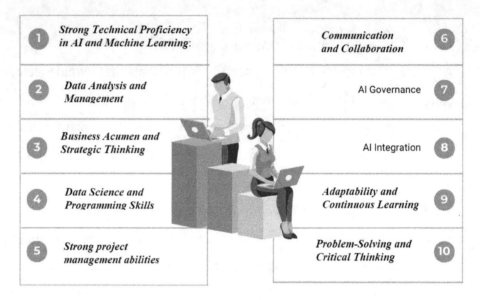

Figure 1.4. Skills Needed for Aspiring AI Consultants

3. *Business Acumen and Strategic Thinking*: Although technical capabilities are important, AI consultants must also have excellent business knowledge. They must understand their customers' industries, business models, and unique difficulties in order to develop AI strategies that correspond with corporate objectives. For example, an AI consultant working with a financial services organization must understand critical financial KPIs, regulatory standards, and market trends in order to build solutions that increase fraud detection or automate financial reporting. Strategic thinking enables consultants to determine how AI may be utilized to address business challenges and add value to their customers.

4. *Problem-Solving and Critical Thinking*: AI consultants typically face challenging challenges that demand innovative solutions. Consultants with strong problem-solving abilities can discover the best AI tools and strategies for addressing specific difficulties. For example, an AI consultant working with a logistics business may need to devise novel ways to improve delivery routes using machine learning algorithms that include traffic patterns, delivery timetables, and fuel economy. Critical thinking is also required for debugging difficulties that develop during AI installation and ensuring that the AI models work as intended.

5. *Communication and Collaboration*: AI consultants must effectively communicate complicated technological concepts to non-technical stakeholders, like executives and managers, to ensure clear and actionable understanding. They must communicate the benefits of AI solutions, as well as the procedures required for deployment and projected outcomes. For example, an AI consultant may need to convey the advantages of utilizing AI-powered customer service chatbots to a company's leadership, ensuring that they understand how it would cut operating expenses while increasing customer satisfaction. AI consultants must also work with cross-functional teams, such as data scientists, IT workers, and business executives, to guarantee smooth AI integration.

6. *Adaptability and Continuous Learning*: As AI evolves, advisors must keep current with new tools and methodologies. Being adaptive and receptive to continual learning enables consultants to stay competitive and provide cutting-edge solutions to their customers. For example, the advent of new technologies such as generative AI (e.g., ChatGPT) or reinforcement learning may create new opportunities for firms, and consultants must be familiar with these trends in order to give appropriate advice. Attending conferences, taking courses, and working on AI research projects are all methods to keep current in the subject.

7. *Strong project management abilities* are essential for AI consultants to keep projects on track across several phases, including planning, design, implementation, and monitoring. They must balance deadlines, resources, and customer expectations while ensuring that AI solutions are delivered on time and under budget. For example, an AI consultant developing an AI-powered fraud detection system for a bank must coordinate with the data science team, IT personnel, and business leaders to ensure that all stakeholders are on board and the project runs successfully. Familiarity with project management tools and processes such as Agile is typically beneficial in this situation.

In general, a successful AI consultant must possess a combination of technical, analytical, and interpersonal abilities in order to traverse the intricacies of AI projects and provide useful solutions to organizations. Mastering these abilities enables consultants to assist firms in realizing the full potential of AI, increasing efficiency and innovation across sectors.

1.4. How AI is driving innovation and transforming industries

AI is driving industry-wide innovation by allowing businesses to streamline operations, improve consumer experiences, and develop totally new business models. Automation is a crucial area of change, with AI-powered solutions simplifying repetitive activities, cutting costs, and increasing productivity. In manufacturing, for example, AI-powered robots and predictive maintenance systems are lowering equipment downtime by identifying faults before they happen. Companies such as Siemens utilize AI to monitor manufacturing machinery in real time, allowing for preventive maintenance that reduces interruptions and improves production efficiency.

In healthcare, artificial intelligence is transforming patient care and medical research. Artificial intelligence algorithms are being used to evaluate massive volumes of patient data, allowing doctors to make more precise diagnoses and personalize treatments. For example, IBM's Watson Health employs artificial intelligence to assess medical literature, patient history, and diagnostic tests, therefore giving clinicians with evidence-based therapy suggestions. Furthermore, AI-powered medical imaging systems can detect illnesses like cancer in their early stages, improving patient outcomes. Hospitals are also utilizing AI to optimize administrative duties such as patient scheduling and resource allocation, hence increasing overall efficiency.

Artificial intelligence is also driving considerable innovation in the retail business. AI solutions, such as recommendation engines and predictive analytics, assist shops in providing tailored purchasing experiences. For example, Amazon's AI-powered recommendation system recommends goods to consumers based on their browsing history and purchase habits, resulting in greater sales and customer happiness. AI-powered chatbots and virtual assistants are also revolutionizing customer service by delivering round-the-clock help, processing common questions, and freeing up human agents to work on more complicated issues. Furthermore, merchants are leveraging AI to optimize inventory management, ensuring that stock levels match customer demand.

AI is also revolutionizing the way banks and financial institutions manage risk, identify fraud, and serve their clients. Artificial intelligence-driven fraud detection systems examine transaction patterns in real time to spot suspicious behavior, assisting institutions such as JPMorgan Chase in preventing fraudulent transactions. AI is also allowing personalized financial services, such as robo-advisors, which utilize machine learning algorithms to deliver individualized investment recommendations. These technologies improve financial services' accessibility and efficiency while lowering operational risks.

Furthermore, AI is having a significant impact on transportation and logistics, notably with the emergence of autonomous cars and route optimization technology. Companies such as Uber and Tesla are developing self-driving cars driven by artificial intelligence, which have the potential to transform personal and commercial transportation. In logistics, AI optimizes delivery routes by taking into account elements such as traffic, weather, and fuel economy. For example, UPS employs AI-powered route optimization software to minimize delivery times and fuel usage, resulting in considerable cost savings and enhanced service.

Agriculture is another field that benefits from AI advancement. Farmers use AI-powered systems to track crop health, adjust irrigation, and forecast harvests. Precision agricultural technology, such as AI-powered drones and sensors, give real-time data on soil conditions and plant health, enabling farmers to make more educated decisions and increase crop output. Companies such as John Deere are employing artificial intelligence to produce self-driving tractors and harvesting equipment, hence increasing agricultural efficiency.

However, artificial intelligence (AI) is driving innovation across sectors by automating processes, enhancing decision-making, and enabling new business models. AI is revolutionizing how organizations function and provide value to their consumers in industries ranging from manufacturing and healthcare to retail, finance, transportation, and agriculture, resulting in higher efficiency, lower costs, and better outcomes.

1.5. Why Choose AI Consulting?

AI consulting is becoming a popular career path due to the increased need for artificial intelligence solutions across sectors. As organizations grasp the importance of AI in driving innovation, enhancing efficiency, and obtaining a competitive advantage, the need for AI consultants grows fast. Choosing a career in AI consulting allows you to work at the cutting edge of technology, assisting firms in integrating AI to solve challenging business challenges and unleash new development opportunities. This job enables experts to change the future of industries by developing and executing AI strategies that are suited to specific business requirements.

One of the primary benefits of AI consulting is the wide variety of sectors it covers. AI consultants can work in a variety of industries, including healthcare, banking, retail, manufacturing, and logistics, applying their knowledge to varied business scenarios. This variation not only keeps the job interesting, but it also gives consultants a diverse skill set that can be used to a wide range of disciplines. For example, an AI consultant may collaborate with a healthcare company on predictive analytics one day and a financial services organization on fraud detection the next. This cross-industry experience contributes to a flexible career path with options to specialize in various areas of AI.

In addition to the variety of sectors, job opportunities in AI consulting are promising due to the ever-increasing need for AI knowledge. AI consultants are in great demand as organizations strive to use AI to improve decision-making, automation, and consumer experiences. According to industry forecasts, the global AI market is likely to expand dramatically in the future years, opening up several chances for consultants to work on cutting-edge projects. Whether working for prominent consulting organizations such as Accenture or Deloitte, or as independent consultants, people in this industry can enjoy attractive job possibilities with room for advancement.

Furthermore, AI consulting provides high work satisfaction since consultants have a direct effect on corporate performance. Implementing AI solutions that optimize processes, decrease costs, and enhance outcomes allows consultants to see actual returns from their efforts. For example, assisting a retail organization with AI-driven inventory management can result in enhanced operational efficiency and profitability, giving the consultant a sense of success. The chance to make a tangible impact in how firms run and compete is a major incentive for people interested in pursuing a career in AI consulting.

Furthermore, AI consulting offers several potentials for ongoing learning and innovation. Artificial intelligence is a constantly growing discipline, with new technology, algorithms, and approaches appearing on a regular basis. As an AI consultant, you are continually exposed to the newest breakthroughs and trends, which keeps you at the forefront of technical innovation. This ongoing learning not only makes the job more intellectually exciting, but it also assures long-term relevance in an industry where remaining current is critical.

Ultimately, AI consulting provides potential career chances, a diversified and dynamic work environment, opportunities to have a significant effect on enterprises, and ongoing learning. As AI continues to transform sectors, the position of AI consultants will become increasingly important, making it an interesting and lucrative career path for people who are enthusiastic about technology and innovation.

Chapter Two
Core AI Knowledge

2.1. AI Fundamentals: Key concepts in AI

Artificial intelligence (AI) comprises a number of core principles that are required to understand how AI systems function and how they might be used to address real-world issues. Machine learning (ML), deep learning (DL), natural language processing (NLP), computer vision (CV), and reinforcement learning (RL) are all key ideas that contribute significantly to AI's capabilities.

Machine Learning (ML) is a key component of artificial intelligence that enables systems to learn and improve based on experience without the need for explicit programming. Machine learning algorithms examine data to detect patterns, generate predictions, and automate decision-making. For example, e-commerce companies utilize machine learning to monitor client behavior and propose items based on browsing history and purchasing trends. In the banking industry, ML algorithms identify fraudulent transactions by evaluating transaction data in real time. Decision trees, random forests, and support vector machines (SVM) are typical techniques in machine learning applications, allowing computers to adapt and change in response to the input they process.

Deep Learning (DL), a branch of machine learning, focuses on neural networks with numerous layers to simulate the human brain's capacity to identify patterns and make judgments. Deep learning has demonstrated great effectiveness in managing massive amounts of data and tackling complicated tasks such as image and speech recognition. For example, deep learning drives face recognition systems that use convolutional neural networks (CNNs) to reliably identify persons. In healthcare, deep learning algorithms analyze medical pictures such as X-rays and MRIs to detect anomalies like cancers with great precision. This technology's ability to handle and comprehend massive volumes of data has far-reaching consequences for a variety of businesses.

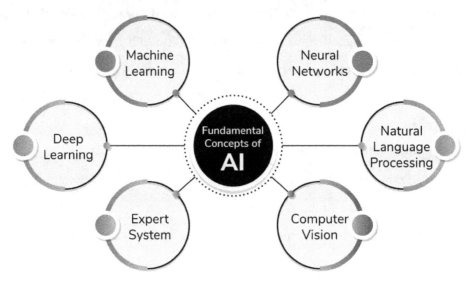

Figure 2.1. Fundamental concept of AI

Natural Language Processing (NLP) allows robots to perceive, interpret, and synthesize human language, resulting in more natural interactions between humans and computers. NLP powers chatbots, language translation services, and virtual assistants like Siri and Alexa. Google Translate, for example, employs natural language processing to translate text between languages by evaluating phrase structure and context. opinion analysis is another NLP application that helps organizations to measure public opinion by analyzing consumer comments from reviews or social media. NLP's capacity to analyze and interpret language improves communication and engagement in a variety of applications.

Computer Vision (CV) enables AI systems to read and comprehend visual information from photos and videos. This technology is critical in fields such as autonomous driving and retail automation. CV is used by self-driving cars to evaluate visual data from cameras, detecting items such as people and traffic lights to ensure safe navigation. CV technology in retail allows for automated checkout systems that recognize and scan items without the need for human participation. The capacity to "see" and comprehend visual information is critical in making AI systems more adaptable and capable of performing complicated tasks that involve visual input.

Reinforcement Learning (RL) is a branch of machine learning in which an agent learns to make decisions by interacting with its surroundings and getting feedback in the form of rewards or penalties. RL has applications in robotics, gaming, and autonomous systems. Google's AlphaGo is a prominent example, since it learnt to play the game of Go by earning rewards for good plays and penalties for mistakes before defeating human champions. In robotics, RL teaches robots how to do tasks like assembly or navigation by optimizing their behaviors via repeated trial and error, resulting in improved performance over time.

Furthermore, data and feature engineering are critical for developing successful AI models. Feature engineering is the process of choosing, changing, or inventing useful features from raw data to improve model performance. In industrial predictive maintenance, for example, raw data like as temperature and vibration are turned into characteristics that aid in the prediction of equipment breakdowns. Effective feature engineering gives AI models with meaningful inputs, which leads to more accurate predictions and better results.

However, as AI systems grow increasingly interwoven into daily life, ethics and prejudice must be addressed. Bias can emerge when AI algorithms learn from data that contains existing prejudices or imbalances, resulting in unfair or erroneous results. For example, facial recognition algorithms trained on non-diverse datasets may perform badly on people with specific skin tones. Addressing these ethical concerns necessitates meticulous data management and algorithm design to assure fairness and accountability. Furthermore, worries about data privacy and the impact of automation on employment emphasize the importance of ethical AI development.

2.2. Machine learning and Deep learning

Machine Learning (ML) and Deep Learning (DL) are two important fields of artificial intelligence (AI) that have transformed the way we process, analyze, and use data to solve complicated issues. Their applicability covers various sectors, changing the way organization's function, and consumers engage with technology.

2.2.1. Machine learning

Machine Learning (ML) focuses on developing algorithms that enable computers to learn from and make judgments based on data without having to be explicitly programmed for each case. ML is frequently divided into three categories: supervised learning, unsupervised learning, and reinforcement learning, each of which addresses a distinct sort of issue.

1. *Supervised learning* involves training an algorithm on a labeled dataset, which means that the input data is accompanied with the proper output. The model learns to link the input to the output, allowing it to make

accurate predictions on previously unknown data. Classification and regression problems are examples of common supervised learning applications. For example, in email spam detection, a model is trained using historical email data tagged as "spam" or "not spam." Over time, the algorithm learns trends (such as keywords or the sender's address) and can accurately detect subsequent spam emails.

Another example is predictive analytics in healthcare, where ML models are used to forecast patient outcomes based on medical history, lifestyle, and genetic information. Machine learning algorithms can forecast the chance of a patient getting a specific ailment based on massive volumes of past patient data, allowing clinicians to act sooner.

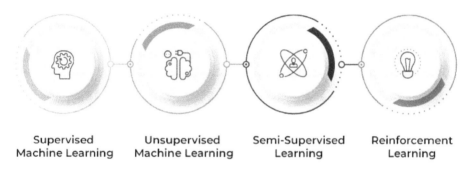

Supervised Machine Learning   Unsupervised Machine Learning   Semi-Supervised Learning   Reinforcement Learning

Figure 2.2. Types of Machine learning

2. ***Unsupervised Learning***: In unsupervised learning, the algorithm works with data that lacks labels, requiring the system to discover structure or patterns in the data on its own. Clustering is a common problem in unsupervised learning, and techniques like as k-means or hierarchical clustering are used to group data points that are similar to one another. This is a typical practice in customer segmentation, in which firms categorize clients based on purchasing behavior or demographics without previous labeling. For example, a retail organization may utilize

unsupervised learning to identify unique consumer groups, allowing them to build customized marketing campaigns based on preferences and purchasing habits.

Another use is anomaly detection in cybersecurity. Machine learning models are used to monitor network traffic and detect anomalous patterns that might signal a security breach. By learning what "normal" network behavior looks like, the system may identify abnormalities such as unexpected surges in data transfer or access from strange places, allowing enterprises to discover and respond to possible threats more quickly.

3. ***Reinforcement Learning (RL)*** is an interactive process in which an agent learns to make decisions by performing actions in a given environment and getting feedback in the form of rewards or penalties. Over time, the agent improves its behavior to maximize the total reward. RL has found substantial uses in robotics, gaming, and self-driving cars. For example, Google's AlphaGo, a reinforcement learning system, learnt to play the board game Go by competing against itself millions of times, perfecting its strategy with each iteration and eventually defeating world champions.

RL algorithms let self-driving cars make real-time driving decisions, such as lane changes and obstacle avoidance, by interacting with their surroundings. The car gets feedback (positive incentives for safe driving and negative penalties for faults such as crashes) and adapts its actions appropriately, gradually increasing its performance.

2.2.2.Deep learning

Deep Learning (DL), a subset of machine learning, extends the notion by utilizing artificial neural networks, which are intended to imitate how the human brain processes information. DL models, particularly those with numerous layers of neurons, are extremely successful at learning from large volumes of unstructured data (e.g., photos, video, and text), eliminating the need for human feature extraction as shown in figure 2.2. This makes deep learning extremely powerful in complicated tasks such as mage recognition, speech processing, and natural language understanding.

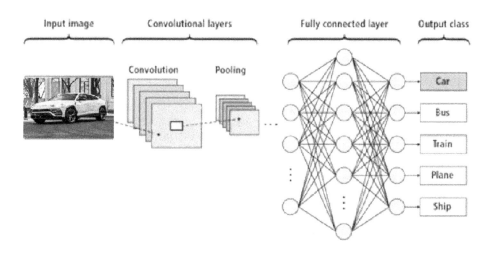

Figure 2.3. Deep Learning Concept.

1. *Convolutional Neural Networks (CNNs)* are a type of deep learning architecture that is especially built for image processing jobs. They excel in processing visual data by using convolutional layers to recognize elements like edges, textures, and objects in an image. CNNs have helped alter areas including healthcare, where they are utilized for diagnostics. For example, CNNs are used to evaluate medical scans (such as X-rays and MRIs) in order to diagnose illnesses like cancer. These devices can highlight problematic spots in scans, allowing radiologists to make faster and more accurate diagnoses.

In the automobile sector, CNNs are critical for self-driving cars to sense their environment. The car's cameras record images of the road, which are subsequently processed by CNNs to detect items such as people, other vehicles, traffic signs, and lane markers, allowing the vehicle to travel safely.

2. ***Recurrent Neural Networks (RNNs) and Long Short-Term Memory (LSTM)*** are two types of deep learning architectures that excel at tasks involving sequential input. Unlike CNNs, RNNs feature a feedback loop that allows them to "remember" past inputs, making them especially effective for context-sensitive jobs. For example, RNNs are employed in voice recognition systems such as those found in virtual assistants (e.g., Siri or Alexa), where the system must comprehend and reply to user requests by analyzing the full phrase rather than individual words.

   LSTM, a kind of RNN, overcomes the constraints of regular RNNs by efficiently handling long-term dependencies, making it excellent for jobs such as language translation and text production. In translation, LSTMs enable a model to comprehend the context of a statement and provide more accurate translations that capture the meaning rather than a word-for-word translation.

3. ***Generative Models (GANs and Variational Autoencoders)***: Deep learning includes generative models such as Generative Adversarial Networks (GANs), which have gained popularity for their capacity to generate new data samples that are like a given dataset. GANs are made up of two networks: a generator and a discriminator, which compete to produce extremely realistic pictures, audio, or video. GANs are utilized in sectors like entertainment and art to produce photorealistic visuals and even new music compositions. GANs, for example, are employed

to produce realistic facial pictures in virtual reality games as well as high-quality textures in 3D modeling.

Variational Autoencoders (VAEs) are another sort of generative model that is utilized for image reconstruction and data reduction. VAEs can develop efficient representations of complicated data, which makes them useful in situations when store space or transmission capacity is restricted.

In general, the primary distinction between machine learning and deep learning is in their approaches to feature engineering and data processing. In machine learning, considerable human involvement is frequently necessary to identify the most important characteristics from the data. For example, with classic machine learning methods such as decision trees or SVMs, data scientists may manually choose certain parameters (such as customer age, purchase history, and geography) to create a prediction model for customer turnover.

On the other hand, deep learning uses neural networks to automate feature extraction. High-level characteristics may be directly learned from raw data by DL models. For example, a deep learning model can automatically identify objects, shapes, and edges in a picture without human assistance when it comes to image categorization. Because it is impossible for humans to manually create features in jobs requiring high-dimensional and unstructured data, DL is especially well-suited for these types of applications.

Deep learning demands far larger datasets and greater processing power than machine learning. Though DL models are more successful with large data and may be used in applications like as voice recognition, autonomous driving, and AI-powered picture analysis, classic ML methods can work effectively with smaller, structured datasets.

2.3.Natural language processing, and computer vision

Two essential fields of artificial intelligence (AI) that allow machines to perceive and interact with the environment in ways that closely resemble human skills are natural language processing (NLP) and computer vision (CV). Whereas CV is focused on the interpretation of visual data, NLP is concerned with producing and comprehending human language. The advancement of AI applications in a variety of sectors, from autonomous systems to healthcare, depends on these two domains.

2.3.1.Processing of Natural Language (NLP)

The area of artificial intelligence known as "natural language processing" gives robots the ability to meaningfully comprehend, interpret, and produce human language. NLP processes both organized and unstructured text data by fusing machine learning and computational linguistics. It is utilized in several applications, including emotion analysis, machine translation, chatbots, and information retrieval systems.

Digital assistants such as Siri, Alexa, and Google Assistant are among the most popular uses of natural language processing (NLP). To comprehend spoken orders and deliver precise, contextually appropriate replies, these systems rely on natural language processing (NLP). If a user requests the weather forecast from a virtual assistant, for instance, the system needs to understand both the user's goal (to know the weather) and the precise location before producing a logical response based on the data it has retrieved.

Machine translation is another common use of natural language processing (NLP), as demonstrated by services like *Google Translate*. By dissecting sentences into individual words, determining the proper grammatical structure, and making sure the output preserves the original meaning, these systems analyze a text in one language and translate it into another. With the advancement of deep learning approaches like transformer models and Bidirectional Encoder Representations from Transformers (BERT), which are excellent at comprehending context and ambiguity in human language, these systems have grown more accurate over time.

NLP is also important in sentiment analysis, which uses computers to assess the emotional tone of text. This is commonly used in customer feedback analysis, in which businesses monitor reviews or social media posts to better understand public perception of their products or services. For example, a corporation may use NLP to evaluate hundreds of customer evaluations and determine if the feedback is good, neutral, or negative, allowing them to make data-driven choices.

However, this involves the use of several mathematical approaches, including; linear algebra, probability theory, statistics, and deep learning. For example, for Text Representation: NLP transforms text into a machine-processable numerical structure. The Bag of Words (BoW) model, which treats each word as a feature in a vector space, is one of the most straightforward methods. The representation of words as dense vectors in continuous vector space is achieved by more sophisticated models such as word embeddings (e.g., Word2Vec, GloVe), which capture semantic meanings by aligning related words closer to one another.

Suppose we have a word embedding space where the vector for the word "king" is v_{king}, the vector for "man" is v_{man}, and the vector for "woman" is v_{woman}. What is the vector v_{queen} based on the analogy "king is to man as queen is to woman" using vector arithmetic?

Therefore, the answer or the word embedding v_{qween} is often computed as:

$$v_{qween} = v_{king} - v_{man} + v_{woman}$$

This method makes use of word connections to deduce new meanings in vector space.

2.3.2.Computer vision (CV)

Computer vision allows robots to analyze and comprehend visual information from their surroundings in the same way that humans can. It includes techniques for analyzing and processing photos and videos in order to recognize objects, people, and settings. CV is a critical component of many AI-powered systems, including self-driving cars, facial recognition, and medical imaging.

CV is crucial in autonomous vehicles since it allows the automobiles to "see" and navigate their environment. Cameras installed on the car collect continuous streams of visual data, which are subsequently analyzed by CV algorithms to recognize road signs, pedestrians, other vehicles, and hazards. For example, Tesla's self-driving cars employ a combination of computer vision and sensor data to make real-time driving decisions, such as stopping for pedestrians or changing lanes based on traffic conditions.

Facial recognition is another important use of computer vision, in which CV systems use facial traits to identify people. This technology is employed in security systems, cellphones, and even social networking sites. For example, Facebook utilizes CV to propose tagging individuals in photographs based on their appearances. On a more secure level, face recognition is used in biometric authentication systems for airport entry control and to unlock cellphones.

CV is transforming the way medical professionals detect and treat illnesses in the realm of medical imaging. To find anomalies like tumors or fractures, CV systems examine medical pictures such as X-rays, MRIs, and CT scans. These tools are extremely useful for early illness identification because they frequently identify patterns or abnormalities that the human eye would overlook. AI-powered systems, such as *DeepMind's* AlphaFold, have demonstrated notable advancements in protein structure prediction, hence bearing substantial consequences for drug development and illness treatment.

2.4.AI Tools and Frameworks

In order for developers, researchers, and companies to effectively design, train, and use artificial intelligence models, AI Tools and Frameworks are essential. The infrastructure, libraries, and algorithms required to expedite the development process—from data preparation to model training and deployment—are provided by these technologies. These are a few of the most popular AI frameworks and tools, along with an overview of their main functions and uses.

1.TensorFlow

One of the most well-known open-source frameworks for deep learning and machine learning applications created by Google is TensorFlow. It offers an all-inclusive environment for creating and utilizing deep neural networks and other machine learning models. Lower-level APIs for more precise control over model construction and training, as well as higher-level APIs (like Keras) for quick prototyping, are both supported by TensorFlow.

TensorFlow, for instance, is frequently used for computer vision applications like image categorization and object recognition. The framework is scalable for big datasets and complicated models since it allows hardware acceleration with GPUs and TPUs. By extending the framework to production settings, TensorFlow Extended (TFX) makes it easier to deploy and maintain machine learning models in pipelines for production.

2.PyTorch

Another potent deep learning framework, PyTorch was created by Facebook's AI Research team and has become rather popular because of its dynamic computational graph and ease of use. PyTorch enables dynamic graph generation, which means the computation is constructed "on the go" during runtime, making it more understandable for developers and researchers than TensorFlow, which initially employed static computational networks. This adaptability is especially helpful in research environments where rapid experimentation is essential.

PyTorch is widely used in NLP tasks such as language modeling, sentiment analysis, and machine translation. It is also simple to work with cutting-edge NLP models like BERT and GPT because of its strong community and support for frameworks like Hugging Face's Transformers. PyTorch is a flexible tool for deep learning applications, as evidenced by its increasing use in academia and business.

3.Keras

Keras provides an API for high-level neural networks. It is user-friendly, expandable, modular, and built to support quick experimentation. With Keras, developers can rapidly prototype models without having to learn the complexities of low-level calculations. Beginners or those who wish to quickly develop a model for research or proof-of-concept reasons will find it particularly appealing due to its clear and straightforward syntax.

For example, Keras is frequently used to create image classification models with pre-trained networks such as Inception or ResNet. Users may load a pre-trained model, make changes, and refine it using their own dataset with just a few lines of code. TensorFlow and Keras combine effortlessly, allowing for scalability as needed.

4.Scikit-Learn

A popular Python package for traditional machine learning techniques is called Scikit-learn. It offers a wide range of tools for data mining and analysis and is based on top of SciPy, NumPy, and matplotlib. Scikit-learn concentrates on conventional machine learning methods like decision trees, support vector machines (SVMs), and random forests, in contrast to TensorFlow and PyTorch, which are designed for deep learning.

One of Scikit-learn's merits is its simplicity and interoperability with the larger Python data science community. It is widely used in regression, classification, clustering, and dimensionality reduction activities. For example, it is a popular toolkit for feature engineering, model selection, and cross-validation in small to medium-sized datasets. It also offers pipelines, which allow users to quickly combine numerous processing processes into a single workflow.

5. Microsoft Azure Machine Learning

Microsoft Azure Machine Learning is a cloud-based platform that offers a comprehensive set of AI capabilities to data scientists and machine learning developers. Azure ML enables customers to create, train, and deploy machine learning models with built-in scalability. It supports popular frameworks such as TensorFlow, PyTorch, and Scikit-learn, making it adaptable for a variety of AI applications.

One important element of Azure ML is its Automated Machine Learning (AutoML) capabilities, which allows developers to automatically search for the optimum model architecture and hyperparameters for a given dataset. It also includes tools for model interpretability, data versioning, and monitoring deployed models, making it suitable for businesses wishing to implement AI into their operations.

6. Google Cloud AI platform

Google Cloud AI Platform provides a variety of services for creating and implementing AI solutions on the cloud. It interacts smoothly with TensorFlow and other machine learning frameworks, including pre-trained models, data labeling tools, and the ability to create bespoke models. It supports AutoML, which enables users to train models on their datasets without requiring extensive machine learning experience.

The platform is frequently used for applications such as image identification, video analysis, natural language processing, and speech-to-text conversion. Its connection with Google's other cloud services, such as BigQuery and Cloud Storage, makes it an appealing alternative for companies wanting to grow their AI workloads in the cloud.

7. IBM Watson

IBM Watson is an AI platform that offers a variety of services for natural language processing, machine learning, and cognitive computing. Watson's API offerings let developers include functions such as speech recognition, language translation, and text analysis in their apps. Watson Studio is a platform product that allows data scientists to create, train, and deploy machine learning models.

Watson's natural language processing (NLP) capabilities are frequently utilized in customer service applications, such as chatbots that interpret and reply to human questions in real time. It also offers document analysis, which enables companies to automate the extraction of useful information from enormous amounts of text.

Generally speaking, AI tools and frameworks are critical for creating and implementing machine learning models, whether for academic or industrial purposes. TensorFlow, PyTorch, and Keras are the most popular deep learning frameworks, whereas Scikit-learn offers a comprehensive collection of tools for classical machine learning. Cloud-based systems such as Microsoft Azure, Google Cloud AI, and IBM Watson provide scalability and pre-built services, making AI more accessible to a wider audience. Each of these tools has distinct characteristics, and selecting the best one relies on needs.

Chapter Three

Identifying AI Opportunities for Businesses

3.1.Introduction

AI is quickly revolutionizing sectors by allowing organizations to streamline operations, enhance consumer experiences, and develop new goods and services. However, in order for enterprises to fully realize the promise of AI, they must first identify the appropriate areas where AI can provide value. Understanding how to identify these possibilities entails understanding where automation, predictive insights, or sophisticated data analysis might improve outcomes.

Examining data-driven, repetitive, or complicated decision-making processes is an important step in discovering AI prospects. For example, in retail, AI may be used for demand forecasting, with machine learning models analyzing previous sales data and industry patterns to estimate future demand. This allows organizations to manage inventories more effectively and save money. Similarly, in the healthcare business, AI is rapidly being employed for diagnosis and personalised treatment suggestions. By analyzing massive volumes of patient data, AI models might help doctors detect trends and forecast possible health problems before they become crucial.

Customer interaction is another important consideration when exploring AI prospects. Businesses use AI-powered chatbots and natural language processing (NLP) tools to automate customer service and give real-time, tailored replies to client inquiries. For example, AI chatbots in e-commerce platforms might propose goods based on a user's browsing history and preferences, therefore enhancing consumer happiness and revenues.

Additionally, AI may assist organizations improve operational efficiency. In manufacturing, AI-powered systems are used for predictive maintenance, which detects equipment defects before they occur, saving downtime and repair costs. Machine learning algorithms evaluate data from sensors mounted on machines to forecast when a component may break, allowing businesses to schedule maintenance in advance.

Identifying AI possibilities entails matching AI capabilities with corporate objectives. This implies that firms must first establish their strategic goals, such as increasing productivity, lowering expenses, or improving customer experiences. Businesses may then assess how AI technology, such as machine learning, computer vision, or natural language processing, might be incorporated to achieve these objectives.

However, identifying AI opportunities requires a combination of understanding data-driven processes, leveraging AI technologies in customer engagement, and aligning AI initiatives with business strategies. By doing so, businesses can unlock AI's full potential and create significant competitive advantages in their industries.

3.2. Understanding How businesses operate and how AI fits in.

A business model outlines how an organization generates, provides, and obtains value. It describes the essential elements that propel an organization's activities, such as its target customer groups, income streams, cost structures, and value offer. Depending on their sector and goals, businesses can operate under a variety of models, including subscription-based, platform-based, or product-sales models. Comprehending these models is crucial in order to discern the ways in which artificial intelligence might augment, optimize, or even revolutionize conventional modes of operation.

Businesses that use a subscription-based business model, such as Netflix or Spotify, make money by charging a regular price for continuous services. This approach benefits greatly from AI as it allows for customized recommendations. For example, Netflix use AI algorithms to examine user viewing patterns and recommend TV series or films based on those choices. In a subscription-based business model, this degree of customisation boosts customer happiness and retention by improving the user experience.

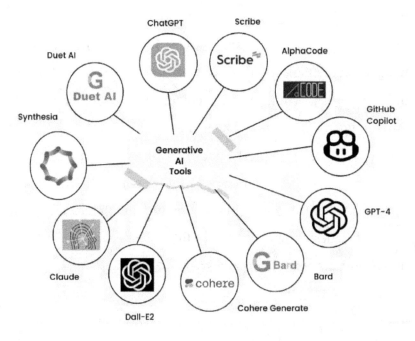

Figure 3.1. AI in Business Operation

Platform-based companies, like *Uber*, *Airbnb*, and *Amazon*, use technology to link buyers and sellers and balance supply and demand. By streamlining user interactions and matching algorithms, AI improves these services. For instance, Uber makes better use of driver availability by using AI to forecast passenger demand based on variables like time, location, and traffic. Furthermore, dynamic pricing is made possible by AI-driven pricing algorithms, which modify rates in real-time in response to supply and demand. This boosts profitability for the business as well as its drivers.

Many companies in the retail and e-commerce sectors use the product-sales model, in which income is derived directly from the sale of products to customers. With better inventory control, demand forecasting, and customer experience, AI may greatly improve this business. For instance, AI-driven chatbots on e-commerce platforms aid with product searches, provide real-time customer support, and even provide tailored suggestions. AI is also used by businesses like Amazon for warehouse automation, which expedites the selecting, packaging, and shipping process and lowers costs while speeding up delivery times.

Reducing operating expenses and optimizing production are two of the main goals of the efficiency-driven business model that manufacturing organizations frequently employ. Process automation and predictive maintenance are how AI integrates into this strategy. To anticipate such problems before they happen, businesses like Siemens and General Electric, for instance, utilize AI to evaluate sensor data from machinery and equipment. This enhances overall production by averting expensive malfunctions and minimizing unscheduled downtime.

AI is being used more and more into financial services sector models that prioritize risk management and safe, effective financial transactions. For instance, a lot of financial organizations, including banks, employ AI to detect fraud. Real-time fraud detection is enabled by machine learning algorithms that examine transaction data to spot unusual trends and indicate possible fraudulent conduct. AI also makes it possible for robo-advisors—like the ones employed by Wealthfront and Betterment—to offer customized investment advice based on a client's financial profile, improving client satisfaction and expanding advisory services.

Business-to-business (B2B) and business-to-consumer (B2C) models are seeing an increase in the use of AI, particularly in marketing and sales. Businesses utilize artificial intelligence (AI) to segment audiences, study consumer behavior, and improve marketing strategies. Businesses can forecast client preferences, optimize pricing, and customize email marketing campaigns with the use of tools like Salesforce's Einstein AI, which increases conversion rates and enhances customer retention.

However, AI may be easily incorporated into a variety of business models by increasing customer satisfaction, streamlining operations, and opening up new income opportunities. AI helps companies to develop and remain competitive in their industries, whether through process automation in manufacturing, dynamic pricing in platform firms, or predictive analytics in subscription services. Comprehending the workings of a business enables organizations to strategically use AI where it may have the greatest impact.

3.3. Analyzing Business Problems with AI Solutions

AI is becoming a vital tool for resolving challenging business issues in a variety of sectors. Businesses may now tackle issues that were previously insurmountable or unmanageable thanks to artificial intelligence (AI), which makes use of data, automation, and sophisticated algorithms. To maximize the value AI can offer, one must be able to identify business challenges and match them with suitable AI solutions. This entails determining the problems, comprehending the data needed, and implementing AI models in line with corporate objectives.

Inefficient processes are among the business issues that AI is most frequently used to address. For instance, businesses frequently encounter difficulties with inventory optimization, demand forecasting, and route planning in the fields of logistics and supply chain management. Businesses may solve these problems with the use of AI-driven solutions like predictive analytics and machine learning models. Amazon, for example, utilizes AI to forecast customer demand based on past data and patterns, improving inventory management by ensuring the appropriate goods are available at the right time. This reduces overstock and stockouts, lowers storage costs, and boosts customer satisfaction with shorter delivery times.

Another big issue that firms confront is customer service bottlenecks. Companies with a large frequency of client interactions frequently struggle to deliver prompt, individualized assistance. AI-powered chatbots and natural language processing (NLP) systems can automate customer care, allowing organizations to answer requests more effectively. Bank of America, for example, utilizes Erica, an AI chatbot, to help clients with banking operations, account queries, and financial advice. This AI system decreases the stress on human customer support agents, reduces response times, and delivers 24/7 assistance, enhancing the overall customer experience.

AI also handles the issue of fraud detection and risk management, particularly in financial organizations. Traditional techniques of identifying fraudulent behavior frequently rely on human procedures and established criteria, which may be sluggish and ineffectual in detecting complex fraud schemes. AI technologies, such as machine learning algorithms, can examine massive volumes of transaction data in real time, detecting abnormalities that may suggest fraud. PayPal employs artificial intelligence to detect suspicious activity in online transactions by evaluating millions of data points every second, therefore preventing fraud before it occurs. This not only enhances security, but also increases consumer trust.

Also, AI handles manufacturing challenges such as equipment downtime and inefficiency. Predictive maintenance is one of the most useful uses of artificial intelligence in this field. By evaluating data from IoT sensors mounted on machinery, AI models may anticipate when equipment will break, allowing businesses to do maintenance proactively rather than reactively. General Electric use AI for predictive maintenance on its industrial assets, decreasing unexpected breakdowns and prolonging the life of costly gear. This AI technology drastically reduces maintenance expenses while increasing operating efficiency.

Marketing optimization is another area where artificial intelligence may help businesses solve difficulties. Companies frequently struggle to determine which marketing initiatives will provide the best return on investment (ROI). AI-powered marketing systems may create targeted marketing campaigns by analyzing customer data such as browsing history, purchase behavior, and social media interactions. AI solutions such as HubSpot and Salesforce Einstein help firms produce targeted marketing, optimize email campaigns, and anticipate client lifetime value. Companies that automate and improve their marketing activities may raise conversion rates, improve client retention, and maximize income.

Employee productivity and resource management are prevalent issues in large firms, as inefficient workflows or time-consuming manual processes can stifle development. AI technologies like Robotic Process Automation (RPA) enable organizations to automate monotonous processes, freeing up staff to focus on higher-value work. UiPath, a renowned RPA vendor, has helped businesses automate tasks such as data input, invoice processing, and payroll administration. AI boosts productivity and lowers operating expenses by cutting down on administrative activities.

However, assessing business problems with AI solutions necessitates a thorough grasp of the issues at hand, the availability of data, and how AI technologies may be implemented successfully. AI offers a wide range of solutions for optimizing operations, improving customer service, identifying fraud, and automating marketing activities, all of which can lead to significant gains in performance and profitability. Businesses that deliberately identify areas where AI may make a difference can solve even the most complicated issues and remain competitive in an increasingly data-driven environment.

3.4. Identifying potential AI use cases within organizations

Identifying AI use cases inside a business starts with understanding how data, automation, and sophisticated algorithms may improve existing processes, address problems, or open up new opportunities. AI's adaptability makes it useful to a wide range of roles, including customer service, operations, marketing, and even human resources. To identify potential AI use cases, organizations must evaluate their current workflows, identify areas that can benefit from predictive analytics, automation, or decision-making capabilities, and determine where AI technologies such as machine learning, natural language processing, or computer vision can add value.

In customer service, for example, AI may be used to shorten response times and improve the client experience. One use case is to utilize AI-powered chatbots to handle regular customer inquiries, freeing up human agents for more difficult issues. For example, H&M uses AI chatbots to help customers monitor orders, answer product-related queries, and resolve frequent concerns. This lowers operating expenses while assuring consumers receive prompt and accurate support, resulting in increased satisfaction and loyalty.

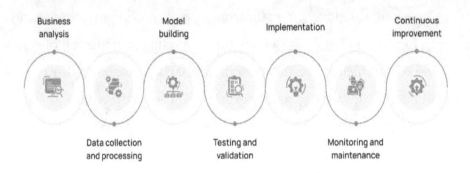

Figure 3.2. Implementing AI in applications

Another crucial area for AI implementation is sales and marketing, where AI can deliver personalized services at scale. AI systems may promote items, optimize marketing campaigns, and personalize content by analysing consumer data such as browsing behaviors, purchase history, and interaction patterns. Spotify, for example, employs machine learning algorithms to build tailored playlists based on each user's listening habits, such as "Discover Weekly". Businesses may utilize AI to categorize audiences, anticipate customer turnover, and uncover cross-selling or upselling possibilities.

Operations and supply chain management provide various prospects for AI applications. AI can help businesses improve inventories, streamline operations, and decrease inefficiencies. For example, in manufacturing, AI-powered predictive maintenance systems monitor equipment in real time and forecast when repair is necessary, avoiding costly downtime. Companies such as Siemens and General Motors have used AI for predictive maintenance to increase machinery longevity, reduce failures, and save maintenance costs.

AI applications may also be found in banking, notably in areas like fraud detection and risk mitigation. Financial institutions may use machine learning to evaluate large volumes of transaction data and find abnormalities that suggest fraudulent conduct. Companies such as PayPal and Mastercard utilize AI algorithms to detect fraud in real time, decreasing losses and boosting client protection. Similarly, AI may help with credit risk assessment, in which computers examine customer data to forecast the possibility of loan defaults, helping banks to make better lending decisions.

AI has the potential to alter HR procedures such as recruiting and personnel management. AI-powered resume screening technologies, for example, can scan and assess massive numbers of applications, allowing HR teams to discover the top applicants more quickly. Companies such as Unilever employ AI in their recruiting process, with AI algorithms analyzing candidates' video interviews, assessing their verbal and nonverbal clues, and predicting their aptitude for jobs. Furthermore, AI may aid in employee retention by detecting trends in performance data that suggest probable turnover, allowing businesses to take proactive measures to boost engagement.

Product development is another interesting field for AI use. AI may be used to accelerate the research and development (R&D) process, assess consumer input for product enhancements, and produce new ideas in response to market trends. IBM Watson, for example, has been utilized by a number of firms to improve product development processes by analyzing enormous datasets, spotting emerging patterns, and recommending new product features that meet user needs.

Ultimately, AI use cases in enterprises may be developed by examining areas where data-driven insights, automation, and predictive capabilities can improve outcomes. Whether in customer service, marketing, operations, finance, human resources, or product development, AI provides solutions that may alter how businesses run, allowing them to be more efficient, create better customer experiences, and remain ahead of rivals. Businesses should make educated decisions about how to incorporate AI into their plans by thoroughly examining existing processes and finding areas where AI might offer value.

3.5. Aligning AI solutions with business goals

To successfully adopt AI within a company, AI solutions must be aligned with the business's overarching strategic goals. This connection guarantees that AI activities immediately benefit the company's growth, efficiency, and competitive advantage. Without this alignment, AI initiatives risk becoming isolated, experimental endeavors that may not provide concrete results. The key to obtaining alignment is to explicitly define corporate objectives and then discover AI solutions that directly address those goals.

For example, if a company's objective is to increase customer happiness, AI may help achieve this by providing tailored experiences and speedier service delivery. A feasible AI solution might involve deploying chatbots using natural language processing (NLP) to provide real-time customer care. Companies such as Sephora have successfully used AI chatbots to provide cosmetic advice and product suggestions based on specific client preferences. This not only enhances the purchasing experience, but it also supports the overall objective of improving consumer pleasure and loyalty.

Another example is in businesses seeking to improve operational efficiency. Businesses in areas such as manufacturing and logistics frequently establish targets to decrease downtime, save costs, and improve operations. AI can help achieve these aims by implementing solutions like predictive maintenance. AI models can forecast when maintenance is necessary based on data from machinery and equipment, averting unexpected breakdowns. This type of AI-driven maintenance, which is employed by corporations such as Rolls-Royce for aviation engine maintenance, helps to improve operations and is closely aligned with the business aim of reducing operational interruptions.

AI may help firms boost income through better decision-making by enhancing data analytics skills. AI technologies, such as machine learning algorithms, may be used to examine vast datasets and get insights into consumer behavior, market trends, and operational performance. Netflix, for example, utilizes AI algorithms to offer material to its customers based on their watching patterns, which not only enhances the user experience but also increases engagement and minimizes churn, resulting in revenue growth.

AI may also support commercial objectives targeted at enhancing risk management. Financial firms, for example, frequently have objectives focused on preventing fraud and controlling credit risk. AI may help achieve these aims by using machine learning algorithms to identify trends in transaction data that indicate fraudulent activity. Companies such as HSBC and JP Morgan employ artificial intelligence to monitor and report questionable transactions in real time, allowing them to accomplish their business objectives of reducing financial risk and preserving consumer assets.

In retail, combining AI with the objective of better inventory management can result in more efficient operations and higher profits. AI-driven demand forecasting systems assist merchants in projecting customer demand based on historical data and seasonal trends. This connection of AI with business goals allows merchants to prevent overstocking or understocking items, lowering costs and boosting sales performance. Zara, for example, utilizes AI to evaluate sales data and alter inventory management appropriately, in line with its objective of minimizing waste while increasing sales.

AI can help organizations focusing on innovation and product development expedite their research and development processes. AI-powered systems may examine consumer input, market data, and industry trends to uncover new product opportunities or improve existing ones. This integrates AI initiatives with the objective of keeping ahead of competition by providing goods that respond to changing market demands. For example, Procter & Gamble use artificial intelligence to evaluate consumer data in order to develop new goods that are in line with their consumers' tastes, therefore generating both innovation and company success.

Hiwever, aligning AI solutions with business goals is essential for ensuring that AI investments deliver real, measurable outcomes. This involves a clear understanding of the company's strategic objectives and identifying how AI technologies can support these objectives. Whether the goal is to enhance customer experiences, improve operational efficiency, increase revenue, or manage risks, AI can be a powerful tool when applied in alignment with the organization's vision and priorities.

Chapter Four

Crafting an AI Strategy for Clients

4.1. Introduction

Developing a complete AI strategy for customers is an important step in assisting organizations in using the power of artificial intelligence to promote development, efficiency, and innovation. As AI becomes an increasingly important component of digital transformation, businesses are turning to experts for advice on how to properly incorporate it into their operations and long-term goals. An AI strategy lays out a plan for discovering high-value AI use cases, aligning AI projects with business objectives, and assuring the effective implementation and scalability of AI solutions.

The first stage in creating an AI strategy is to understand the client's business goals and obstacles. This includes doing a detailed examination of the company's industry, target market, and competitive environment to determine where AI can have the greatest impact. For example, a retail company may use tailored marketing to increase consumer engagement and sales, whereas a manufacturing company may use predictive maintenance to maximize output and decrease downtime. By integrating AI with the client's unique goals, the approach guarantees that AI activities directly contribute to business results.

Next, evaluate the client's present technological infrastructure and data ready. AI solutions are strongly reliant on high-quality data, thus knowing the client's data sources, storage systems, and data management methods is critical. For example, if a financial institution wants to employ

AI for fraud detection, they must guarantee that their transaction data is available, clean, and formatted in such a manner that AI algorithms can efficiently evaluate it. This step frequently entails finding holes in the existing data infrastructure and advocating enhancements, such as implementing cloud-based platforms or improving data governance procedures.

Once the client's objectives and infrastructure have been identified, the next stage is to identify AI use cases based on their potential effect and practicality. AI consultants collaborate with customers to discover particular areas where AI may help address issues or create new possibilities, such as automating repetitive operations, improving decision-making through data analysis, or improving consumer experiences with tailored suggestions. Prioritization ensures that the customer concentrates on high-impact initiatives that can yield immediate results while building the groundwork for future more complicated AI implementations.

A critical component of any AI plan is assessing the resources and skill required for execution. To enable effective adoption of AI efforts, specialist skills in machine learning, data science, and software engineering, as well as change management knowledge, are frequently required. For example, a healthcare provider deploying AI for diagnostics will require both technical specialists to design and maintain AI models and healthcare professionals to incorporate the solutions into clinical procedures. The plan should describe how the customer may either develop in-house AI capabilities or work with external suppliers to acquire the requisite skills.

Another critical component of designing an AI strategy is creating a detailed plan for AI governance and ethics. As AI systems become more incorporated into decision-making processes, questions of transparency, fairness, and bias must be addressed. For example, when using AI in recruiting procedures, organizations must guarantee that the algorithms are devoid of prejudice to avoid unfair hiring practices. An successful AI plan contains rules for assessing AI performance, resolving ethical problems, and assuring compliance with applicable legislation.

An AI plan should include a road map for implementing AI solutions throughout the firm. Once the first AI initiatives have been successfully implemented and demonstrated value, the next stage is to broaden their use across departments or functions. For example, a corporation that has successfully used AI for supply chain efficiency may expand its use to inventory management or demand forecasting. The plan should describe how AI efforts may be expanded and incorporated into the overall business strategy, allowing the firm to develop and remain competitive.

However, developing an AI strategy for clients is a multi-step process that includes aligning AI with business objectives, assessing data and infrastructure readiness, identifying use cases, and resolving talent, governance, and scalability concerns. A well-defined AI strategy not only assists customers in effectively implementing AI technologies, but also prepares them for long-term development and innovation in an increasingly AI-driven environment.

4.2. Developing an AI strategy aligned with business goals

Developing an AI strategy that matches with business objectives is critical for ensuring that AI efforts add actual value and contribute to the organization's overall development and success. This approach include gaining a thorough grasp of the company's strategic objectives, identifying important areas where AI may have an influence, and ensuring that AI solutions closely complement these goals. An AI strategy that is not linked with the company's goals might result in wasted money, unused technology, and lost opportunities.

The first step in aligning an AI strategy with business goals is to establish a defined set of objectives. For example, a retail organization may want to enhance sales by enhancing consumer involvement. In this example, the AI strategy may focus on adopting machine learning-powered recommendation systems to give clients with individualized product recommendations based on their previous purchases and browsing history. Amazon has effectively employed this method to increase sales by providing tailored suggestions, which is consistent with the company's objective of maximizing revenue through consumer customisation.

Another example is in financial services, where a bank may want to save operating expenses while increasing client service. An AI strategy aligned with this purpose may include the use of AI-powered chatbots to address regular customer questions. This not only minimizes the need for human customer support workers, but also allows clients to obtain immediate replies around the clock. Banks such as HSBC and Bank of America have used AI chatbots to simplify customer service, lowering costs while increasing customer experience.

Once the business objectives are clearly defined, the next stage is to discover particular AI use cases that directly support these goals. AI may help a manufacturing organization enhance operational efficiency by optimizing predictive maintenance. By analyzing sensor data from equipment with machine learning algorithms, AI can anticipate when gear is likely to malfunction, allowing for prompt maintenance and eliminating costly downtime. General Electric (GE) has successfully deployed AI-based predictive maintenance to guarantee that its industrial equipment runs effectively, in line with its business aim of reducing operational disruptions.

In the healthcare business, an AI strategy might be tailored to improve diagnosis accuracy and patient outcomes. For example, AI-powered diagnostic systems that analyze medical pictures can aid in the earlier detection of illnesses such as cancer. Hospitals and clinics are rapidly employing AI to improve diagnostic skills, which is directly related to their objective of enhancing patient care and results. IBM's Watson Health platform, for example, employs AI to aid in cancer detection, allowing clinicians to make more educated judgments and supporting healthcare providers' overall objective of enhancing treatment efficacy.

To enable successful alignment between AI projects and business goals, use cases must be prioritized based on their potential impact and practicality. Not all AI efforts will yield immediate results, so concentrating on activities that can immediately demonstrate value helps generate momentum. For example, a logistics business seeking to optimize delivery routes might begin by using AI-driven route optimization algorithms that examine traffic patterns, weather conditions, and delivery timetables. This is closely aligned with the objective of lowering fuel costs and improving delivery times, as evidenced by organizations such as UPS through AI-driven logistics optimization.

To ensure successful alignment between AI initiatives and business goals, it is critical to prioritize use cases based on potential impact and feasibility. Not all AI projects may deliver immediate returns, so focusing on initiatives that can quickly demonstrate value helps build momentum. For example, a logistics company with a goal to optimize delivery routes can start by implementing AI-driven route optimization algorithms that analyze traffic patterns, weather conditions, and delivery schedules. This aligns directly with the goal of reducing fuel costs and improving delivery times, as companies like UPS have demonstrated with their AI-driven logistics optimization.

Scalability and long-term company objectives are also important considerations for a successful AI strategy. While first AI implementations may focus on addressing urgent difficulties, the strategy should be structured to expand throughout the enterprise. For example, a retail organization may start utilize AI for inventory management, but as the strategy matures, AI may be used to other areas such as customer segmentation, demand forecasting, or marketing automation. This guarantees that AI solutions continue to meet the company's changing objectives throughout time.

However, ensuring that the appropriate governance and ethical frameworks are in place is crucial to building an AI strategy that is aligned with corporate objectives. As AI becomes more integrated into decision-making processes, it is critical that these systems are transparent and consistent with the company's ethical norms. To avoid discriminatory practices, a financial institution that uses AI for loan approvals must guarantee that the algorithms are bias-free. Establishing governance frameworks ensures that AI systems are consistent with the company's overall principles and regulatory standards, therefore supporting both short- and long-term commercial objectives.

Furthermore, building an AI strategy that aligns with business goals necessitates a thorough knowledge of the company's objectives, prioritizing high-impact AI use cases, assuring scalability, and applying ethical standards. Companies can guarantee that their AI investments produce value and contribute to long-term success by closely tying AI projects to business goals, such as improving customer experience, lowering costs, or increasing operational efficiency.

4.3. Building a Data-Driven Culture

Data is the foundation of every effective AI approach. To effectively use AI, firms must first establish a data-driven culture in which choices are made based on data insights rather than intuition or tradition. A strong data culture helps enterprises to fully grasp the potential of AI technology, as AI models rely significantly on access to high-quality data to deliver meaningful insights. This change toward data-driven decision-making necessitates not just investing in the appropriate technology, but also cultivating an organizational attitude that views data as a strategic asset.

To foster a data-driven culture, it is critical to stress the value of data at all levels of the business. Leaders have an important role in illustrating how data may enhance decision-making, increase efficiency, and reveal new business prospects. For example, Netflix's whole recommendation engine is based on data analysis, allowing it to offer individualized content to its viewers, increasing consumer happiness and retention. This emphasis on data-driven insights is deeply embedded in Netflix's corporate culture, since data is continually crucial to product choices, marketing tactics, and even content development.

Another critical step in developing a data-driven culture is making data available and clear to all workers. While technical teams like as data scientists and AI engineers play an important role in evaluating and using data, everyone in the business, from marketing to operations, should be enabled to use data in their everyday tasks. Companies may invest in self-service data tools and dashboards, which enable employees to readily access and comprehend data. For example, Google encourages its employees to use internal data tools to track key performance indicators (KPIs) and optimize procedures. By democratizing data, Google assures that any team member can participate in data-driven decision-making.

One of the obstacles in developing a data-driven culture is breaking data silos, which are the habit of various departments keeping onto data without sharing it throughout the firm. To overcome this issue, businesses should establish policies and tools that encourage data sharing and cooperation. For example, Procter & Gamble (P&G), a worldwide consumer products corporation, created a data-sharing ecosystem to break down barriers and guarantee that insights from marketing, supply chain, and product development departments were in sync. By fostering cross-functional data access, P&G was able to enhance decision-making processes and optimize operations.

In addition to technologies and infrastructure, cultivating a data-driven culture necessitates training and upskilling individuals to work successfully with data. Many firms have implemented data literacy programs to teach their employees how to read, analyze, and use data insights. For example, Airbnb established a company-wide data literacy training to guarantee that workers at all levels could use data to make educated decisions. The training included everything from fundamental data interpretation to advanced data science approaches, allowing non-technical employees to participate to data-driven projects. As a result, Airbnb evolved into a more data-driven business, with insights guiding choices in areas like as pricing optimization and customer experience.

Furthermore, building a data-driven culture requires prioritizing data governance and ethical data use. As AI and data analytics grow more prevalent, it is critical to have frameworks in place to handle data appropriately. Companies such as Microsoft have created sophisticated data governance systems to protect data privacy, security, and adherence to legal requirements like the GDPR (General Data Protection Regulation). This not only assures ethical data usage, but also builds confidence among workers and consumers, underlining the importance of data in strategic decision-making.

Finally, rewarding data-driven wins helps to build a culture in which data is valued. When data-driven projects provide concrete business results, such as greater revenue, more customer happiness, or lower expenses, it is critical to publicize these accomplishments. This emphasizes the significance of data and encourages continued adoption of data-centric methods. For example, Zynga, a gaming firm, credits much of its success to data-driven decisions, often providing case studies of how data analytics has resulted in better game design or more efficient marketing methods.

Therefore, developing a data-driven culture is critical for maximizing the value of AI methods. It entails gaining leadership support, democratizing access to data, breaking down silos, upskilling people, and encouraging responsible data usage. When data is integrated into the organization's fabric, AI technologies may perform to their full potential, driving innovation, enhancing decision-making, and providing commercial success.

4.4. AI Implementation Plan

Developing an efficient AI implementation strategy is crucial for ensuring that AI projects are completed within a reasonable period and with adequate resources. Setting explicit timetables, defining the necessary resources (such as staff, technology, and data), and developing quantifiable milestones to track progress at each step of the project are all part of an AI implementation strategy. Without a well-structured strategy, AI initiatives face the danger of being delayed, overbudget, or failing to produce the promised results.

The first stage in developing an AI implementation strategy is to establish a realistic schedule that takes into consideration the challenges of AI deployment. AI projects usually include phases including data gathering and preparation, model creation, testing, deployment, and continuing monitoring. For example, if a company is developing an AI-powered fraud detection system for financial transactions, the timeline should include data collection (which could take weeks or months depending on the volume and quality of the data), model training and validation (which could require several iterations to optimize), and system deployment (including integration with existing infrastructure). Each of these stages should have clearly defined start and finish dates, as well as buffers for unanticipated issues.

To avoid delays, allocate suitable resources from the start. AI initiatives need a combination of technical and business skills, including data scientists, AI engineers, software developers, and business analysts. For example, while developing an AI-powered customer support chatbot, the technical team would create the natural language processing (NLP) model, while business analysts would verify the chatbot's replies were consistent with the company's brand and customer engagement objectives. Furthermore, access to high-quality data is critical, therefore data engineers may be required to guarantee the data is clean, organized, and formatted for AI model training purposes. Ensuring that these jobs are filled before the project begins will assist in avoiding bottlenecks later in the process.

Identifying milestones to track progress and keep the project on track is an important part of AI project planning. Milestones act as checkpoints, allowing the team to assess progress, modify schedules, and reallocate resources as needed. For example, key milestones in developing an AI-powered inventory management system for a retail company could include the completion of the data integration phase (where historical sales data is collected and prepared), the delivery of the first model prototype (an early version of the AI system that predicts inventory needs), and the final model deployment (when the system is fully operational and integrated with the company's ordering system). Each milestone should have clearly stated success criteria, such as attaining a specific degree of forecast accuracy or assuring system stability.

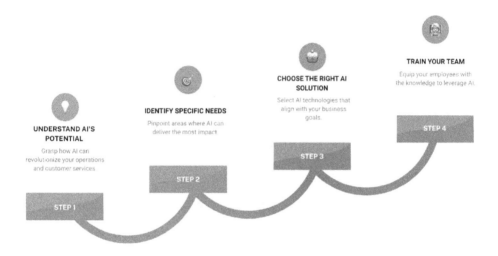

Figure 4.1.. Implementing AI

It's also critical to incorporate flexibility into the implementation strategy. AI initiatives sometimes include some degree of uncertainty, particularly when it comes to modeling performance. For example, when constructing a machine learning model for predictive maintenance in a manufacturing facility, initial models may not attain the required accuracy in forecasting equipment breakdowns. This would need more iterations to develop the model, which might lengthen the schedule. Incorporating flexibility into the implementation strategy allows the team to resolve such challenges without derailing the project.

Furthermore, creating testing and validation milestones is critical to ensuring that the AI system achieves its objectives. For example, when implementing an AI-based recommendation system for an e-commerce platform, an important milestone would be to do A/B testing to see how the AI-driven suggestions compare to the previous system. This phase allows for iterative changes based on user feedback, and testing results must be carefully examined to see whether the AI solution is ready for full-scale implementation.

However, a comprehensive AI implementation strategy includes post-deployment goals such as evaluating the AI system's performance in real-world scenarios and resolving any difficulties that develop. In a hospital setting, for example, after installing an AI system to help doctors diagnose illnesses, the strategy should include frequent assessments of the system's diagnostic accuracy, user input from healthcare experts, and upgrades based on fresh medical data. Continuous performance monitoring guarantees that the AI solution continues to add value and is adaptable to changing situations or new data sources.

Furthermore, a successful AI implementation strategy relies on precise timetables, adequate resource allocation, and well-defined milestones. Organizations may guarantee that their AI efforts are completed on time, within budget, and in line with business objectives by breaking the project down into manageable parts and tracking progress at each level. Examples of AI-based customer service systems, fraud detection tools, and predictive maintenance show how careful design may improve the effectiveness and scalability of AI installations.

4.5. Addressing Challenges in AI Adoption

Adopting AI technology poses a number of problems for enterprises, ranging from technical complications to cultural opposition. Understanding and resolving these difficulties early on is critical for effective AI integration. The most typical challenges that businesses encounter when deploying AI are data quality and availability, a lack of AI competence, interaction with legacy systems, and cultural opposition. However, with the correct techniques and approaches, these challenges may be solved.

One of the most major barriers to AI adoption is the lack of data quality and availability. AI algorithms rely on enormous amounts of high-quality data to make accurate predictions and provide insights. If the data is inadequate, inconsistent, or biased, the AI results may be wrong or misleading. For example, if the data utilized to construct AI models for credit risk assessment is skewed against specific demographic groups, loan choices may be made unfairly. To overcome this issue, firms should invest in strong data governance structures that guarantee data is clean, organized, and fair. They can also employ data augmentation techniques to create synthetic data when real data is insufficient or constrained.

Another prevalent difficulty is a lack of AI competence within the organization. Many businesses lack the necessary in-house personnel, such as data scientists, AI engineers, or machine learning specialists, to effectively create and deploy AI solutions. This skills mismatch might delay down AI initiatives or result in underperforming models. To address this issue, firms might engage in AI training and upskilling initiatives to strengthen internal skills. Google, for example, offers the Google AI for Everyone program, which teaches employees of all skill levels how to comprehend and interact with AI technology. Companies can also collaborate with AI consulting firms or engage external AI professionals to provide the knowledge required for specific projects.

Integration with old systems is yet another key hurdle for firms implementing AI. Many industries, particularly in banking and healthcare, use old technology that is incompatible with new AI technologies. This can impede data access, processing, and the deployment of AI models. For example, in the healthcare industry, integrating AI-driven diagnostic tools with current electronic health record (EHR) systems is sometimes a difficult task due to incompatible data formats and fragmented systems. To solve this, enterprises may use middleware solutions to bridge the gap between old systems and AI platforms, or they can update their IT infrastructure in stages to enable easier AI integration.

Cultural opposition is another significant impediment to AI adoption. Employees may be hesitant to embrace AI technology because they are concerned that it may replace their employment or disrupt the way they operate. Workers in the manufacturing industry, for example, may be resistant to the implementation of AI-driven predictive maintenance systems because they fear that automation would eliminate the need for human intervention. To solve this obstacle, firms must prioritize change management and effectively explain the benefits of AI. They should underline that AI is intended to supplement, not replace, human talents, and that it may result in more meaningful, less monotonous work. Furthermore, businesses may involve workers early in the AI adoption process by teaching them on how AI will enhance their responsibilities, thereby easing concerns and encouraging buy-in.

As companies depend more heavily on AI for important decision-making, ethical and regulatory concerns about AI are growing. The possibility of bias, a lack of transparency in AI models (also known as the "black box" problem), and worries about data privacy can also hinder AI adoption, particularly in areas such as banking or healthcare where regulatory compliance is rigorous. For example, AI models used in credit scoring must be visible and explainable in order to assure fairness and regulatory compliance. To overcome this issue, firms must establish AI ethical frameworks that stress justice, transparency, and responsibility in AI systems. Furthermore, they can employ explainable AI (XAI) methodologies to make AI model judgments easier to understand for regulators and end users.

However, while enterprises confront major problems during AI adoption, these obstacles may be overcome with the correct solutions. Businesses may effectively deploy AI technologies to boost innovation and enhance productivity by guaranteeing data quality, eliminating the AI skills gap, integrating AI with legacy systems, cultivating a supportive company culture, and resolving ethical issues. Overcoming these obstacles not only sets the route for effective AI adoption, but also guarantees that AI will become a significant addition to the organization's long-term goals.

Chapter Five

Data Management and Preprocessing

5.1. Introduction

Data management and preparation are crucial elements in any AI or machine learning project because they ensure that the data utilized is high quality, well-structured, and fit for model training. The effectiveness of an AI model is frequently determined not just by the algorithms but also by how effectively the data is prepared. Data management include handling, storing, and organizing data, whereas data preparation is concerned with cleaning, converting, and formatting data before it is fed into a model. Even the most powerful algorithms might yield inferior results if data is not properly managed and preprocessed.

Data management begins with the gathering and storage of data. In today's digital age, businesses may access vast volumes of data from a variety of sources, including databases, IoT devices, social media, and consumer interactions. To manage this data successfully, you must first establish the necessary data storage infrastructure, such as data warehouses or cloud-based storage solutions. Companies must also implement data governance rules to protect data privacy, security, and compliance with requirements such as the General Data Protection Regulation (GDPR). A solid data management strategy provides the foundation for successful data preparation.

After data collection and storage, the following stage is data preparation, which ensures that the data is clean, consistent, and ready to be analyzed. Preprocessing often includes a number of activities, such as data cleansing, missing value management, data normalization, and feature engineering. For example, when developing an AI model to predict customer turnover, data preparation might include filling in missing values (e.g., incomplete customer records), deleting duplicate entries, and translating categorical variables such as "gender" or "region" to numerical form. These methods contribute to the elimination of data noise and inconsistencies, which might otherwise decrease model performance.

Data normalization or standardization is an important element of preprocessing, particularly when working with characteristics of varying sizes. For example, in a model forecasting house prices, data such as "number of rooms" and "square footage" may be on dramatically different scales, making it difficult for the model to accurately assess their value. The model can better grasp the associations between these characteristics if they are normalized (i.e., transformed to a comparable scale).

Another key consideration is featuring selection and dimensionality reduction. In many circumstances, not all of the characteristics in a dataset are applicable to the task at hand. Irrelevant or duplicated features can introduce noise and complexity into the model, lowering its performance. For example, when forecasting loan defaults, "age" and "income level" may be more essential than less relevant data such as "email domain." Data dimensionality can be reduced using techniques such as Principal Component Analysis (PCA), which retains just the most important information.

However, data management and preparation are critical elements in the AI development pipeline, ensuring that data is not only safely kept but also optimal for machine learning algorithms. Organizations may increase the accuracy and dependability of their AI systems by cleaning, normalizing, and selecting the right features. This leads to better decision-making and commercial results.

5.2. Importance of Data in AI

Data is the foundation for artificial intelligence (AI) development. Even the most advanced AI algorithms will fail to produce meaningful results if their data is of poor quality. In AI, models discover patterns and make predictions based on the data on which they are trained, hence data quality, quantity, and relevance are crucial to the model's performance. The significance of data in AI is analogous to the role of gasoline in an engine: no matter how sophisticated the engine, it cannot run without high-quality fuel.

One of the key reasons for data's importance in AI is that it serves as the raw material from which models learn. For example, in image identification tasks, vast datasets of annotated photographs are used to train AI models to recognize specific items like cats, vehicles, and buildings. If the dataset is too limited or inadequate, the model may fail to generalize successfully, resulting in inaccurate predictions. Real-world examples include autonomous driving, where businesses such as Tesla and Waymo train their AI systems using enormous datasets of road conditions, vehicle interactions, and environmental elements. The more data the model has, such as different driving circumstances and road situations, the stronger the AI's navigation and decision-making capabilities.

Data quality is also an important consideration in AI. A model is only as good as the data it is trained on, therefore making sure the data is clean, impartial, and reflective of the real-world scenario is critical. For example, if an AI model used in a healthcare application to forecast illnesses is trained on data that mostly reflects one demographic group, its predictions may be inaccurate when applied to other demographic groups. This problem, known as data bias, can result in unethical and unjust conclusions. To address this, healthcare AI systems must use varied, representative datasets that appropriately reflect the larger population's age, gender, color, and health problems.

The amount of data is equally significant. In machine learning, the more data a model has access to, the better it learns complicated patterns and makes accurate predictions. This is especially true in deep learning, where models are built to recognize detailed patterns in large datasets. For example, in natural language processing (NLP), models like OpenAI's GPT-4 are trained on massive volumes of textual data from a variety of sources, including books, websites, and forums. This large-scale data allows the model to create human-like text answers on a wide range of topics while also understanding linguistic subtleties, which would be impossible with smaller datasets.

Furthermore, real-time data is critical for certain AI applications, such as fraud detection in financial services. Fraud detection systems rely on real-time data to identify suspicious transactions and prevent fraud. AI models in this sector must constantly examine real-time financial transaction data in order to discover abnormalities that might suggest fraud. PayPal, for example, uses artificial intelligence systems to evaluate millions of transactions in real time, indicating possibly fraudulent activity within seconds. The speed and accuracy of these systems are completely dependent on the availability and quality of real-time data.

However, data is the lifeblood of AI systems, helping to train, validate, and improve models. High-quality, diversified, and abundant data allows AI models to train more efficiently, make accurate predictions, and provide important insights across a wide range of applications. From self-driving vehicles to healthcare and financial services, the value of data in AI cannot be understated. Using the appropriate data at the right scale enables enterprises to realize the full promise of AI and drive innovation in their industry.

5.3. Data Collection and Integration

Data gathering is the first critical stage in creating AI models and decision-making systems. It entails acquiring relevant and high-quality data from many sources to serve as the basis for model training, analysis, and insight production. Effective data collecting methods guarantee that AI systems have the essential information to execute tasks like prediction, categorization, and decision-making. Surveys, sensors, social media monitoring, transactional data, and public databases are all suitable for diverse use cases.

For example, in the retail industry, organizations gather data through customer surveys, purchase histories, and website analytics to acquire insights into consumer behavior. By gathering this information, merchants may utilize AI to forecast shopping trends, offer tailored items, and improve inventory management. Another example is in smart cities, where data is collected via IoT devices to monitor traffic patterns, pollution levels, and energy use. Artificial intelligence systems can combine and analyze this data to improve city planning, decrease energy waste, and better control traffic flow.

After the data has been obtained, the next stage is data integration, which entails merging data from various, sometimes divergent, sources into a single format for analysis. Integration is critical since many firms have siloed data across departments or systems, resulting in fragmented insights and lost opportunities. Data integration tools like ETL (Extract, Transform,

Load), APIs, and data lakes assist to integrate this data, allowing AI models to gain a comprehensive perspective of the information.

A prominent example of data integration may be seen in the healthcare sector, where patient data is frequently dispersed across many systems such as electronic health records (EHRs), lab findings, and imaging databases. ETL operations extract diverse data from many sources, transform it into a consistent format, and load it into a central repository. Once linked, AI models may use the aggregated data to forecast patient outcomes, offer treatment regimens, and detect early symptoms of illness. Companies such as IBM Watson Health employ this strategy to aggregate massive volumes of healthcare data, improving the accuracy and efficiency of AI-driven tests and treatments.

APIs (Application Programming Interfaces) are another important tool for data integration. APIs provide easy data sharing between multiple systems and platforms, making it easier to collect real-time data from a variety of external sources. For example, in financial services, banks and fintech businesses utilize APIs to combine transactional data from various accounts and platforms, providing AI models with a comprehensive perspective of user activity. This information may then be utilized to give tailored financial advice or identify potential fraud.

When dealing with huge amounts of unstructured data, data lakes provide an effective option for data integration. A data lake is a centralized repository where businesses may keep raw data in its original format until it is suitable for analysis. This is especially important in businesses like media and entertainment, where data in several formats—such as text, video, and audio—must be handled. Platforms such as Netflix employ data lakes to combine user viewing histories, content choices, and social media involvement, allowing their AI systems to offer highly tailored content to users.

However, good data collection and integration are critical to the success of AI programs. Whether acquiring data via IoT sensors in smart cities or integrating consumer data across retail platforms, enterprises must use the proper methodologies to create a comprehensive and reliable dataset. Businesses that effectively integrate diverse data sources may use AI to unearth new insights and make data-driven choices across several industries.

5.4. Data Cleaning and Preprocessing

Data cleaning and preprocessing are critical processes in preparing data for successful machine learning and AI applications. These processes are critical because they directly impact the accuracy, quality, and performance of AI models. Properly cleansed and preprocessed data guarantees that the insights gained are trustworthy and useful.

1. *Missing Values*: Dealing with missing values is one of the most typical data cleansing challenges. Missing data can arise for a variety of reasons, including mistakes in data input or incomplete surveys. For example, in a dataset containing customer information, some entries may have missing values for age or income. Imputation is one method for dealing with missing values, in which missing entries are replaced by statistical values such the mean, median, or mode. For example, if a property pricing dataset has missing square footage numbers, they can be approximated using the median value of other properties in the same neighborhood.

3. *Remove Duplicates*: Duplicate entries can distort the findings of any study. For example, in a dataset tracking employee performance, multiple entries for the same individual might result in erroneous judgments.

Duplicates are removed by finding and removing redundant records. To simplify this job, Python tools such as pandas include methods like drop_duplicates(). Keeping each record unique contributes to the analysis's veracity.

4. ***Normalizing and Scaling Data***: Normalization and scaling are approaches for bringing disparate characteristics into a similar range. This is especially crucial for distance-based algorithms like k-nearest neighbors or support vector machines. For example, if a dataset includes parameters such as wealth (in thousands) and age (in years), their ranges may be very different. Normalizing these values to a similar scale, such as 0 to 1, ensures that each feature contributes equally to the model. Common methods for this purpose include min-max scaling and standardization (z-score normalization).

5. ***Encoding Categorical Variables***: Most machine learning methods require numerical input. Categorical variables, such as 'gender' and 'city', must be transformed to numerical representations. One typical approach is one-hot encoding, which converts each category to a binary column. For example, the 'city' column with values ['Kuala Lumpur', 'Tripoli', 'London'] would be split into three binary columns: is Kuala Lumpur, is Tripoli, and is London. This strategy facilitates the effective interpretation of categorical data by algorithms.

6. ***Handling Outliers***: Outliers have a substantial influence on the performance of machine learning models. An outlier is a data point that deviates considerably from the other observations. For example, given a dataset of student test results, a score of 1000 may be considered an outlier if the bulk of values are less than 100. Outliers can be detected using statistical approaches like the Interquartile Range (IQR) or visualization

techniques like box plots. Outliers can be removed or transformed, depending on how they affect the dataset.

7. *Data Transformation*: Data transformation is the process of altering data in order to increase its quality or fulfill analysis criteria. For example, with time series data, timestamps may need to be transformed into a more usable format before extracting attributes such as the day of the week or month. Furthermore, applying log transformation to skewed data can assist to stabilize variance and make it more regularly distributed.

8. *Feature Engineering*: Feature engineering is the process of adding new features or changing existing ones to improve model performance. For example, in a dataset for predicting home values, additional features such as 'house_age' can be produced from the 'year_built' feature. Creating relevant features that represent the underlying patterns in the data may greatly improve model accuracy.

Generally, data cleaning and preprocessing are critical processes in developing strong and reliable AI models. Data scientists can ensure that their models are built on high-quality, reliable data by addressing missing values, removing duplicates, normalizing data, encoding categorical variables, handling outliers, transforming data, and engineering features. This leads to improved performance and more insightful results.

5.5. Data Privacy and Security

In the digital era, data privacy and security are key components of securing personal and corporate information. As organizations increasingly rely on massive volumes of data to make decisions, the requirement to safeguard and responsibly manage this data has become critical. it privacy concerns people' rights to their personal information, including how it is acquired, processed, and disseminated. In contrast, data security refers to the technological and administrative protections that protect data from breaches, theft, and unauthorized access.

Data privacy is becoming increasingly important as technology progresses, and more data is created. Consumers are more conscious than ever of how their personal information is used, saved, and shared. Maintaining data privacy not only fosters consumer trust, but it is also a legal necessity under rules such as the European Union's General Data Protection Regulation (GDPR) and the United States' California Consumer Privacy Act (CCPA). These rules provide tight criteria for how organizations should manage personal data, such as gaining consent, guaranteeing openness in data gathering, and granting individuals the ability to view or remove their data.

GDPR, for example, requires organizations to seek explicit consent before collecting any personal data, as well as explicitly describe how the data will be processed. Failure to comply with these requirements can result in hefty fines, like Google's €50 million penalty for not being honest with consumers about how their data was used for targeted advertising.

Data security refers to the safeguards put in place to keep data safe from unauthorized access, cyberattacks, and possible breaches. These safeguards vary from encryption, in which data is encoded and only accessible with the correct decryption key, to firewalls and intrusion detection systems, which monitor and prevent illegal access. Organizations also use multi-factor authentication (MFA) to guarantee that only authorized persons have access to sensitive information.

For example, banking companies frequently utilize encryption to secure sensitive consumer data such as credit card numbers and account information during transactions. Furthermore, multi-factor authentication guarantees that even if a password is hacked, an extra layer of protection (such as a text message code or fingerprint scan) prohibits unauthorized access.

5.5.1. Data Maintenance Challenges Privacy in AI.

With the growth of AI and machine intelligence, data is more valuable than ever, but it also poses new privacy issues. AI models frequently rely on enormous datasets that may include sensitive or personal information. A specific source of worry is AI's capacity to draw conclusions or predictions from this data, often exposing more about individuals than they initially agreed to give.

For example, facial recognition technology has prompted privacy concerns. These AI-powered systems can identify people from enormous collections of photos, which are frequently taken without authorization. Several towns in the United States, notably San Francisco, have outlawed the use of face recognition by police enforcement owing to privacy concerns and potential abuse.

In response to privacy issues in AI, new solutions are developing that allow enterprises to exploit data while remaining private. Differential privacy is one such strategy, which involves introducing statistical noise to data in order to prevent individual information from being identifiable while still enabling relevant analysis. Federated learning is another way in which AI models are trained across decentralized devices (such as smartphones), guaranteeing that data remains on the user's device rather than being shared.

Apple's iOS is an excellent example of differential privacy in operation. By using differential privacy, Apple may gather and analyze use patterns from millions of users to enhance their products while protecting individual users' information. Beyond compliance with legal rules, corporations must evaluate the ethical consequences of their data handling practices. Transparency in how data is used and shared is critical for establishing confidence. Companies should emphasize ethical data management, ensuring that AI systems do not propagate prejudice or mishandle sensitive information.

The Cambridge Analytica incident is a famous example, in which Facebook data was exploited for political objectives without users' consent. This breach of trust underlined the necessity for organizations to implement better data protection standards, as well as the need of making ethical decisions when dealing with personal information.

However, as the world becomes increasingly data-driven, preserving data privacy and security is critical for protecting individuals and enterprises. Businesses may secure sensitive information while promoting innovation and sustaining confidence in the digital economy by implementing strong security measures, complying with privacy legislation, and remaining honest with consumers.

Chapter Six
Building and Deploying AI Models

6.1. Introduction

Building and implementing AI models necessitates a methodical strategy that converts raw data into useful insights and solutions. The process begins with comprehending the problem and setting the objectives, which then lead the selection of relevant data and methods. Data preparation, model building, and deployment are the three key steps of this journey, and each is important to the AI system's success. The initial stage in developing an AI model is data preparation. This includes gathering pertinent data, cleaning it to remove errors or inconsistencies, and prepping it to ensure it is in an acceptable format for analysis. Normalization, addressing missing values, and encoding categorical variables are all possible data preparation steps .For example, in a project forecasting customer attrition, data preparation may include cleaning transaction logs, standardizing client demographics, and encoding categorical variables such as customer status.

After the data has been prepared, the next step is model creation. This includes selecting and training algorithms to learn from the data. Machine learning models can range from basic linear regressions to complicated neural networks, depending on the problem's complexity. A recommendation system, for example, may use collaborative filtering techniques, whereas image recognition tasks could make use of convolutional neural networks. Model development also includes analyzing and refining the model to ensure it works well on previously unknown data, including measures such as accuracy, precision, recall, and F1 score.

The final step is to incorporate the model into a real-world application or system. This entails transforming the model into a production environment capable of making real-time predictions or judgments. Deployment might include providing APIs, integrating the model into existing software systems, or developing user interfaces for interacting with the model. For example, adopting a fraud detection model may entail connecting it with a financial transaction processing system to detect suspicious activity as it occurs.

Effective deployment also requires monitoring and updating the model to ensure its long-term performance. This includes tracking metrics, retraining the model with fresh data, and adapting to changes in the underlying data distribution or business needs. For example, if a model used to forecast loan defaults begins to decrease in performance, it may require retraining with more recent data to account for changing financial patterns.

However, developing and implementing AI models is a multifaceted process requiring a combination of data science, software engineering, and domain knowledge. Each stage—from data preparation to deployment—is critical to ensure that AI models provide accurate and relevant insights, resulting in better decision-making and increased operational efficiency.

6.2. Model Selection and Training

Model selection and training are critical elements in creating successful AI solutions. The nature of the problem, the type of data available, and the project's unique objectives all influence the methods and approaches used. Making the appropriate decisions at this stage may have a big influence on the performance and efficiency of the AI model.

Model selection begins with a knowledge of the problem and determining the type of data at hand. For classification jobs that require categorizing data into preset classifications, techniques such as Logistic Regression, Decision Trees, Support Vector Machines (SVM), and more complex models such as Neural Networks can be used. For example, in a spam email categorization system, Logistic Regression may be utilized due to its simplicity and interpretability, however more sophisticated models such as Convolutional Neural Networks (CNNs) may be used if the feature set contains text pictures.

Algorithms such as Linear Regression, Ridge Regression, and more advanced models such as Gradient Boosting Machines (GBMs) or Neural Networks are useful for regression problems that need continuous value predictions. For example, when predicting real estate values, Linear Regression may be used for its simplicity, or more complicated models such as Random Forest Regressors to capture non-linear correlations in the data.

Clustering methods like as K-Means, Hierarchical Clustering, and DBSCAN (Density-Based Spatial Clustering of Applications with Noise) can be used to group comparable data points together in the absence of predetermined labels. Customer segmentation in marketing is an example of how K-Means clustering may assist identifying separate groups of customers based on their purchase behavior.

Model training entails applying the selected algorithm to the data and refining its parameters to improve performance. This procedure usually involves dividing the data into training and validation sets to examine how well the model generalizes to new data. For example, while training a Neural Network for picture identification, techniques like backpropagation and gradient descent are used to change the network's weights, reducing the discrepancy between expected and real labels.

Hyperparameter adjustment is also an important part of model training. It entails changing parameters that govern the learning process, such as the learning rate, the number of layers in a neural network, or the number of trees in a Random Forest. Grid Search or Random Search, for example, can assist in determining the ideal combination of hyperparameters that results in the greatest model performance.

The choice of algorithm and the training process are influenced by factors such as the complexity of the problem, the amount of data available, and the computational resources. For example, deep learning models, which are strong but computationally costly, may be saved for issues involving huge datasets and complicated patterns, such as picture or speech recognition, whereas simpler techniques may be more suited for smaller datasets.

In summary, model selection and training are essential for developing effective AI solutions. Data scientists may create models that provide accurate and actionable insights by carefully selecting algorithms that are appropriate for the task and utilizing rigorous training processes. This rigorous method assures that the AI system works effectively in real-world circumstances while also addressing the task's particular demands and problems.

6.3. Model Evaluation and Testing

Model assessment and testing are critical steps in the machine learning lifecycle, ensuring that the produced model works effectively and satisfies the intended criteria prior to deployment. This procedure comprises evaluating the model's accuracy, robustness, and generalizability using a variety of methodologies, including validation and cross-validation.

Model evaluation often begins by dividing the dataset into separate subsets to determine how well the model works on previously unknown data. The most frequent strategy is to divide the data into three sets: training, validation, and test. The training set is used to fit the model, the validation set aids in the tuning of the model's hyperparameters, and the test set assesses its overall performance.

One important statistic for measuring model accuracy is accuracy, which quantifies the proportion of right predictions out of all forecasts produced. Metrics like Precision, Recall, F1 Score, and ROC-AUC (Receiver Operating Characteristic - Area Under the Curve) might give more information on classification challenges. For example, in a medical diagnostic system, high precision guarantees that the model correctly predicts a condition, and high recall ensures that the majority of real instances are diagnosed.

Metrics used for regression tasks include Mean Absolute Error (MAE), Mean Squared Error (MSE), and R-squared. MAE quantifies the average size of prediction errors, MSE penalizes greater mistakes more harshly, and R-squared represents the model's share of variance explained. For example, in forecasting house prices, MSE might be used to punish bigger differences between anticipated and real prices, ensuring that the model is correct throughout a wide range of forecasts.

Validation is the process of tuning and adjusting the model's hyperparameters using a distinct dataset. A prominent approach is k-fold cross-validation, which divides the data into k subsets or "folds." The model is trained on k-1 folds, then verified on the remaining fold. This method is done k times, with each fold acting as a validation set once. The findings are then averaged to provide a more reliable approximation of the model's performance. For example, a 10-fold cross-validation evaluates the model's performance ten times, reducing the danger of overfitting and providing a more trustworthy measure of accuracy.

Leave-One-Out Cross-Validation (LOOCV) is a subset of cross-validation in which each data point acts as a validation set only once. This approach is very beneficial for tiny datasets, although it can be computationally intensive. In contrast, stratified cross-validation guarantees that each fold is reflective of the total class distribution, which is especially crucial for unbalanced datasets.

Hyperparameter adjustment is frequently used with cross-validation to improve model performance. Grid Search and Random Search are two techniques for methodically exploring alternative hyperparameter combinations in order to discover the optimum set that improves the model's accuracy. Grid Search, for example, might experiment with different learning rates and regularization parameters to determine the best configuration for a neural network.

Model performance evaluation also includes analyzing the model's resilience and capacity to generalize to new, previously unknown data. Techniques such as confusion matrices give a thorough assessment of the model's performance by displaying true positives, true negatives, false positives, and false negatives. Additionally, learning curves may assist show how the model's performance changes with changing training data quantities, offering insights into whether the model is underfitting or overfitting.

In general, model assessment and testing are critical for ensuring that machine learning models are accurate, dependable, and can generalize to real-world data. By applying approaches like validation, cross-validation, and multiple performance measures, data scientists may rigorously analyze and update their models, finally offering robust AI solutions that fulfill the specified performance standards.

6.4. AI Model Deployment

Deploying AI models into production environments is a vital stage in the machine learning lifecycle, moving them from experimental to functioning solutions that provide real-world value. This method includes various best practices to guarantee that models work consistently, connect easily with existing systems, and deliver accurate forecasts over time.

1. *Model Validation and Testing*: Thorough validation and testing of an AI model is required prior to deployment. This includes verifying that the model works effectively not only on training and validation data, but also on previously unknown production data. Testing should cover a variety of scenarios that mimic real-world settings and edge cases. For example, a recommendation system implemented in an e-commerce platform should be evaluated with diverse user behaviors to guarantee it can handle many sorts of product searches and interactions.

2. *Scalability and Performance*: The deployment environment must support the model's scalability to accommodate changing loads and performance requirements. This includes selecting the appropriate infrastructure, such as cloud-based solutions or on-premises servers, that can scale resources up or down in response to the amount of requests. For example, a model for real-time fraud detection in financial transactions should be put on a scalable cloud platform capable of handling large transaction volumes and providing quick reaction times.

3. *Integration with current Systems*: To ensure successful deployment, the AI model must be seamlessly integrated with current systems and workflows. This frequently entails creating APIs (Application Programming Interfaces) that allow the model to interact with other software components. For example, a sentiment analysis model for evaluating customer comments should relate to the company's CRM

(Customer Relationship Management) system so that customer profiles are automatically updated depending on sentiment ratings.

4. **Monitoring and Maintenance**: Once implemented, AI models must be continuously monitored to ensure that their performance and accuracy remain consistent over time. This includes monitoring parameters like forecast accuracy, reaction times, and system health. Automated monitoring systems and dashboards can help discover problems early on. For example, a predictive maintenance model used in manufacturing should be monitored for departures from expected performance in order to resolve any issues as soon as they develop.

5. **Handling Model Drift**: Over time, the data distribution and environment in which the model runs might change, resulting in a phenomenon known as model drift. To guarantee that the model stays accurate and relevant, it must be retrained and updated on a regular basis using fresh data. For example, a recommendation system may require frequent retraining to adapt to changing user preferences and market trends.

6. **Security and Compliance**: Data privacy and security are critical considerations when using AI models. Ensure that the implementation complies with legal regulations and industry standards, such as GDPR for data protection. Encryption, access limits, and secure data processing techniques can help protect sensitive information. For example, in healthcare applications, models that handle patient data must conform with HIPAA (Health Insurance Portability and Accountability Act) to ensure patient confidentiality.

7. **Documentation and Version Control**: Proper documentation of the model's deployment procedure, configuration, and dependencies is critical for preserving clarity and making future upgrades easier. Version control systems assist manage different iterations of the model and

codebase, allowing for rollbacks if problems develop. For instance, utilizing technologies like Git to track code changes and model versions guarantees that teams can track updates and revert to previous versions if necessary.

8. *User Training and assistance*: Successful implementation requires training and assistance for end users and stakeholders. Ensure that users understand how to engage with the AI model, evaluate its results, and resolve any difficulties that may emerge. For example, educating customer service representatives to utilize a chatbot successfully can improve their capacity to help consumers and answer issues quickly.

However, implementing AI models in production requires a multifaceted strategy that encompasses validation, scalability, integration, monitoring, and security. By adhering to these best practices, businesses can guarantee that their AI models provide consistent performance, connect seamlessly with current systems, and continue to give new insights and capabilities over time.

Chapter Seven

AI Consulting Tools and Platforms

7.1. Introduction

Consultants play a critical role in assisting firms through the complexity of artificial intelligence (AI) adoption. To successfully negotiate these hurdles and create effective solutions, AI consultants use a wide range of technologies and platforms. These tools are required at various phases of the AI lifecycle, such as data management, model building, deployment, and continuous monitoring. Understanding the scope and capabilities of these technologies is critical for consultants to deliver important insights and achieve the best results for their customers.

AI Development Platforms provide the foundation for creating, training, and deploying AI models. Platforms such as Google Cloud AI Platform, Microsoft Azure Machine Learning, and Amazon SageMaker provide a comprehensive collection of services that help with every stage of an AI project. These systems offer scalable cloud infrastructure, integrated development environments, and pre-configured machine learning algorithms. For example, Google Cloud AI Platform interfaces smoothly with TensorFlow and AutoML, allowing consultants to quickly create and deploy models suited to specific business requirements. These platforms make the development process easier by including powerful tools for model training, assessment, and deployment.

Data Management Tools are essential for ensuring that the data utilized in AI projects is clean, relevant, and well-organized. Tools such as Apache Hadoop, Apache Spark, and Databricks excel in managing massive datasets and performing complicated data processing tasks. Databricks, for example, combines the power of Apache Spark with a collaborative environment, enabling teams to manage large amounts of data effectively and do complex analytics. Effective data management is critical for developing accurate and trustworthy AI models because it guarantees that the data fed into them is of high quality and correctly structured.

Machine Learning Frameworks are essential for building and training AI models. TensorFlow, PyTorch, and Scikit-Learn are three frameworks that provide a diverse set of tools and libraries for implementing machine learning algorithms. TensorFlow, developed by Google, is well-known for its flexibility and scalability in deep learning applications, whereas PyTorch is popular for its simplicity of use and dynamic computational graph capabilities. These frameworks include pre-built functionalities and model structures that speed up the development process, making it easier for consultants to construct advanced AI solutions.

Data visualization and analysis tools are essential for evaluating and presenting AI results. Tableau, Power BI, and Matplotlib allow consultants to build interactive dashboards and rich visualizations. For example, Tableau enables users to create attractive visual reports that effectively convey complicated data findings to stakeholders. Visualization tools are critical for transforming AI model outputs into actionable insights, enabling data-driven decision-making, and proving the value of AI solutions to customers.

Collaboration & Workflow AI project management requires the use of tools to ensure successful communication among team members. Jupyter Notebooks, GitHub, and Slack facilitate collaboration by providing real-time code sharing, version control, and project management. Jupyter Notebooks enable the creation and sharing of live code, equations, and visualizations, whilst GitHub facilitates version control and collaborative work. Slack enables real-time communication, allowing teams to coordinate activities and handle difficulties quickly.

Model Monitoring and Management Tools are critical for ensuring the performance and correctness of AI models after deployment. Tools like MLflow and Prometheus allow you to track model performance, manage model versions, and monitor metrics. MLflow provides a framework for managing the whole machine learning lifecycle, from experiment tracking to model deployment. Prometheus supports real-time monitoring and alerting, ensuring that models continue to function as intended and that any abnormalities are addressed swiftly.

However, AI consulting tools and platforms are critical for the effective implementation of AI initiatives. They offer the infrastructure and functionality required for data administration, model creation, deployment, and monitoring. AI consultants may use these technologies to increase their productivity, create high-quality solutions, and achieve substantial outcomes for their customers.

7.2. AI Platforms for Consultants

Cloud-based AI platforms have transformed the area of artificial intelligence by offering scalable, adaptable, and powerful tools for creating, implementing, and managing AI systems. For consultants, these platforms are crucial because they provide a full portfolio of services and capabilities that simplify the AI lifecycle and improve project outcomes. Google Cloud AI, Amazon Web Services (AWS) AI, and Microsoft Azure AI are among the leading companies in this field, with each offering unique capabilities and benefits.

Google Cloud AI is well-known for its comprehensive array of AI and machine learning capabilities that help to expedite the development process. One of its most notable aspects is TensorFlow, a Google-created open-source machine learning framework that supports complicated neural network models and deep learning applications. Google Cloud AI also provides AutoML, a tool that automates the process of developing machine learning models, allowing consultants to generate unique models without considerable coding experience. For example, a consultant working with a retail client may utilize Google Cloud AI tools to create a recommendation engine that personalizes product recommendations based on consumer behavior, employing AutoML to speed up model training and deployment.

Amazon Web Services (AWS) AI offers a full array of AI services via the AWS cloud platform, which is renowned for its scalability and integration capabilities. Amazon SageMaker is a standout service, providing a fully managed environment for developing, training, and deploying machine learning models. SageMaker offers built-in algorithms, automatic model adjustment, and simple deployment choices. For example, a consultant may use SageMaker to create a predictive maintenance model for a manufacturing customer by analyzing sensor data and forecasting equipment faults. AWS AI also includes services such as Amazon Rekognition for image and video analysis and Amazon Lex for conversational interface development, broadening the breadth of AI solutions consultants may provide.

Microsoft Azure AI is notable for its integration with Microsoft's vast range of productivity and business applications. Azure Machine Learning is an essential component, offering a variety of services for developing, training, and deploying machine learning models. It provides automated machine learning to simplify model creation, as well as Azure

Cognitive Services, which contains pre-built APIs for natural language processing, computer vision, and speech recognition. For example, a consultant working with a healthcare provider may utilize Azure Cognitive Services to create a solution that collects and analyzes patient information from medical records, employing natural language processing capabilities to improve data quality and accessibility.

In addition to these fundamental services, all three platforms— Google Cloud AI, AWS AI, and Microsoft Azure AI—provide substantial support for data storage and administration, allowing consultants to easily manage massive amounts of data. They also offer tools for model monitoring and administration, ensuring that AI solutions stay effective and up to date after implementation. For example, a consultant may utilize Google Cloud AI's monitoring tools to follow a machine learning model's performance in real time or use AWS CloudWatch to set up alerts and view model accuracy and performance data.

Overall, cloud-based AI systems provide consultants with a vast array of tools and services, each with its own set of strengths and capabilities. By leveraging these platforms, consultants may provide new and effective AI solutions that are personalized to their customers' individual needs, increasing value and improving business outcomes across several sectors.

7.3. AI Project Management Tools

Effective project management is crucial for the success of AI initiatives, given their complexity and the need for seamless coordination among various stakeholders. AI project management solutions with the necessary features to coordinate projects, monitor progress, and guarantee on-time delivery are Jira, Asana, and Trello. Each tool has unique capabilities designed to address various facets of project management, assisting teams in maintaining organization and goal focus.

Figure 7.1. AI Project Management

Jira is well known for its strong project management skills, especially when it comes to Agile projects. Jira is a well-known issue tracking, sprint planning, and backlog management tool that was created by Atlassian. Jira helps teams working on AI projects to efficiently prioritize activities, track progress using configurable workflows, and break down complex jobs into manageable problems. Jira, for example, may be used by an AI project team working on a predictive analytics model to handle tasks including feature engineering, data gathering, model training, and validation. The platform's usefulness in organizing different project components and guaranteeing team member alignment is further enhanced by its integration with other technologies, such Confluence for documentation and Bitbucket for version control.

Asana has a simple UI and a variety of project management capabilities that help to optimize processes and boost team communication. It supports task assignments, due dates, project timeframes, and progress monitoring using visual boards and Gantt charts. Asana may be used in AI projects to define and manage project milestones, allocate tasks to team members based on their expertise, and track the success of various phases such as model building, testing, and deployment. For example, a team developing an AI-powered chatbot may utilize Asana to handle conversational design, natural language processing integration, and user testing. Integration with other productivity tools, including Slack and Google Drive, improves communication and file sharing, resulting to a more efficient project management process.

Trello is well-known for its simple and visual approach to project management, which uses boards, lists, and cards. It is especially useful for organizing activities and tracking progress in a highly visual and easy way. Trello enables teams to construct boards for various stages of a project, such as planning, progress, and completion, with cards representing specific tasks or deliverables. Trello may be used in AI projects to organize activities such as data pretreatment, model validation, and deployment. For example, a team working on an image recognition system may use Trello to divide activities into distinct lists, track the status of each job, and ensure that all areas of the project are going as expected. The tool's versatility and ease of use make it a popular choice for teams seeking a straightforward solution for task management and collaboration.

However, Jira, Asana, and Trello each provide distinct advantages for managing AI projects. Jira excels in managing complicated Agile projects, with thorough issue tracking and integration features. Asana offers a broad set of project management capabilities, with a focus on collaboration and visual progress monitoring. Trello provides a straightforward, visual approach to task management, making it ideal for teams seeking an intuitive and adaptable solution. By utilizing these technologies, AI project teams may increase productivity, streamline procedures, and achieve successful project outcomes.

7.4. Collaboration and Communication Tools

Collaboration and communication technologies have transformed the way teams operate, giving platforms for effective engagement and project management. Aside from Slack, Microsoft Teams, and Asana, there are several additional programs that cater to distinct elements of cooperation, each with its own set of capabilities that contribute to overall efficiency and effectiveness.

Slack is well-known for its flexibility in communication. It offers a wide range of connectors with other programs, like Google Drive, Trello, and Zoom, which improves its usefulness and helps teams optimize their workflows. Slack's usage of channels helps to organize talks by subject or project, minimizing clutter and making it simpler to monitor important conversations. The option to utilize emoticons, gifs, and threads provides a more casual and engaging element to team communication, perhaps improving morale and cohesiveness.

Microsoft Teams stands out because of its extensive set of capabilities that interact with Microsoft 365. It provides comprehensive video conferencing features, making it an excellent choice for virtual meetings and webinars. The platform's connection with apps including as Word, Excel, and PowerPoint enables users to collaborate on documents in real time without moving between tools. Teams' emphasis on collaboration extends to the ability to set up shared workspaces where team members may collaborate on projects, exchange files, and measure progress.

Asana is particularly useful for project management. Its user-friendly interface enables teams to establish projects, assign tasks to team members, and define due dates and priority levels for each. Features such as task dependencies, timeframes, and project dashboards give insight into progress and possible obstacles. Asana also integrates with other applications like Slack and Google Calendar, which increases its value for managing workflows and scheduling.

Other famous apps include Trello, which organizes tasks and projects using a card-based structure. Trello's visual approach lets organizations organize processes and measure progress using boards, lists, and cards, making it ideal for visual learners and teams that value structured but flexible task management. Basecamp provides a full array of features such as to-do lists, milestone tracking, and group chat, with the goal of reducing the need for several applications by unifying diverse project management capabilities into one location.

Google Workspace (previously G Suite) is another important collaboration platform, including cloud-based apps such as Google Docs, Sheets, and Slides. These solutions enable several people to modify documents at the same time, allowing for real-time collaboration and eliminating version control difficulties. Google Workspace's interaction with other Google services, such as Gmail and Google Meet, provides a unified experience for communication and file management.

Git and platforms such as GitHub and GitLab play an important role in software development. Git's version control system enables numerous developers to work on the same codebase at the same time, thanks to features such as branching and merging, which promote collaborative development and code integrity. GitHub and GitLab improve this by providing extra functions like issue tracking, code review, and continuous integration, making them essential for modern software development teams.

Finally, Zoom and Cisco Webex provide specialized video conferencing solutions necessary for virtual meetings, webinars, and remote collaboration. These applications offer high-quality video and audio, as well as screen sharing and recording possibilities, to help in distant communication and collaboration.

The success of collaboration and communication technologies is determined by their correct deployment and the team's adaptability to their features. By properly utilizing these technologies, teams may increase productivity, streamline communication, and achieve their goals more efficiently.

7.5.AI Prototyping Tools

AI prototype tools are intended to speed up the creation and presentation of artificial intelligence solutions, allowing teams to swiftly present their concepts and solutions to clients. These technologies simplify the process of developing AI demos by providing user-friendly interfaces and pre-built components, potentially reducing development time and expenses.

Microsoft Azure Machine Learning is a popular artificial intelligence prototype tool. This platform includes a variety of tools for developing, training, and deploying machine learning models. Its drag-and-drop interface, known as the Azure Machine Learning Designer, enables customers to create machine learning processes without requiring considerable code. This capability is very beneficial for fast creating prototypes and presenting them to customers since it allows the rapid integration of various machine learning components and algorithms.

Google Cloud AI Platform is another effective tool for AI prototyping. It provides a range of services that address different stages of the AI development lifecycle, from data preparation to model deployment. Google's AutoML features enable users to build unique machine learning models with little coding knowledge. These automated technologies speed up the creation of AI prototypes, allowing teams to create and test models rapidly and effectively.

IBM Watson Studio is also famous for its artificial intelligence prototyping capabilities. Watson Studio offers a complete platform for data scientists and developers to create, train, and maintain AI models. Its toolkit offers a variety of pre-built models and visual tools that make it easier to create prototypes. The connection with IBM's Watson services, such as natural language processing and image identification, enables the quick creation of demos that may be tailored to highlight certain AI capabilities.

Google's Dialogflow is a useful tool for individuals interested in natural language processing and conversational artificial intelligence. Dialogflow provides an easy-to-use interface for creating chatbots and conversational agents. It supports numerous languages and works with a variety of messaging systems, making it perfect for quickly developing and presenting AI-powered conversational solutions. Its pre-built agents and customisable features enable the quick creation of interactive demos.

Streamlit is a recent technology that is becoming popular for developing interactive machine learning and data science applications. It makes it simple to construct web-based apps using Python code, allowing developers to easily generate and display AI models and data visualizations. Streamlit's simplicity and flexibility to create live demos make it a powerful tool for showcasing AI solutions in a compelling and interactive manner.

RapidMiner is another platform that facilitates AI development, with an emphasis on data-science workflows. Its visual interface enables users to create and run machine learning models without requiring considerable programming experience. RapidMiner's data preparation, model training, and assessment features enable the quick development of prototypes that can be easily shared with clients for feedback and validation.

Also, Jupyter Notebooks offer a flexible platform for creating and presenting AI models. Jupyter Notebooks, while not a specific prototype tool, are commonly used because they allow you to integrate code, graphics, and narrative prose in a single document. This makes them an ideal tool for building interactive demos and presenting the findings of AI studies in a style that is understandable to both technical and non-tech stakeholders.

Generally, AI prototyping tools are critical for the quick creation and presentation of artificial intelligence solutions. Using these technologies, teams may quickly create and exhibit prototypes, allowing for efficient client demos and feedback. The type of AI solution being built, as well as the unique demands of the project, influence the tool being developed and the desired level of interactivity and customization.

Chapter Eight

Working with Clients as an AI Consultant

7.1. Introduction

Working with clients as an AI consultant requires knowing both the technical components of artificial intelligence and the client's unique business requirements. An AI consultant serves as a link between complicated AI solutions and practical commercial applications, guiding companies through the hurdles of adopting and integrating AI technology. This necessitates not just a thorough understanding of AI technologies like machine learning, natural language processing, and data analytics, but also the ability to explain these concepts effectively to non-technical stakeholders.

The first step in engaging with customers is to understand their company objectives and difficulties. As an AI consultant, it is critical to engage with clients in talks that explain their goals, pain areas, and expectations for AI solutions. This exploration phase assists in determining the exact areas where AI may provide value, such as automating procedures, boosting customer interaction, or obtaining insights through data analysis. The ability to listen carefully and ask the proper questions is critical during this phase, as it guarantees that the offered AI solutions are consistent with the client's company goal.

After determining the client's requirements, the next stage is to create and present an AI solution. This entails transforming corporate concerns into AI initiatives that produce measurable solutions. As an AI consultant, you must be able to convey complicated AI principles in simple words, with an emphasis on how the technology may help the client overcome their issues. Whether you're offering predictive analytics, image recognition, or a chatbot, it's critical to demonstrate to the customer how AI can increase productivity, enhance decision-making, and generate new income. Creating a prototype or demo may be an effective method to demonstrate potential solutions and increase confidence in your approach.

Once a solution has been decided upon, the implementation step begins. Technical experience is required because you will be in charge of building, testing, and implementing AI models or systems. Throughout this phase, contact with the customer is crucial. Keeping the customer informed about progress, possible hurdles, and milestones helps to keep them involved and happy with the project's direction. Regular updates and feedback loops can also assist in fine-tuning the solution and ensure it fulfills the client's expectations.

The need for post-implementation assistance for AI consultants working with customers is sometimes ignored. AI systems must be constantly monitored, maintained, and optimized to guarantee they function as intended over time. It is critical to educate the customer on the iterative nature of AI initiatives and the importance of ongoing assistance. This might include training internal teams, establishing performance criteria, and giving regular updates as the AI system improves with fresh data.

However, working with clients as an AI consultant necessitates a combination of technical expertise, communication skills, and commercial acumen. The consultant may not only provide excellent AI solutions, but also walk customers through the complexity of AI adoption, ensuring that the technology is in line with their company objectives. Building solid connections, managing expectations, and producing outcomes that illustrate

AI's revolutionary potential are all critical components of success in this profession.

8.2. Understanding Client Needs

Understanding client demands is a vital step in providing successful AI solutions, and conducting in-depth client interviews is one of the most effective methods for doing so. As an AI consultant, the purpose of these conversations is to obtain a thorough knowledge of the client's business difficulties, goals, and particular areas where AI might add value. A well-structured interview process can assist identify not only stated demands but also latent opportunities that the client may be unaware of. This necessitates a combination of technical knowledge, strategic thought, and effective communication abilities.

One of the initial approaches for conducting customer interviews was to ask open-ended questions that prompted the client to comment on their business processes and pain issues. Instead of asking, "Do you need AI to automate a process?" a better question is, "What are the main challenges your team faces in managing day-to-day operations?" This style of inquiry assists the consultant in understanding the larger context and identifying places where AI may have the most impact. It also allows for the discovery of previously overlooked inefficiencies or difficulties.

Another key strategy is to delve deeply into the client's data habits. AI solutions frequently rely on huge datasets, and data quality and availability are critical to the success of AI initiatives. During the interview, inquire about the sorts of data the client gathers, how it is kept, and if it is organized or unstructured. For example, asking, "What kind of data are you currently collecting, and how do you use it?" might assist determine whether the customer has the data architecture required for AI deployment. If data challenges are discovered, the project may change its attention to improving data collecting and administration before using AI solutions efficiently.

By asking forward-thinking questions, you may also learn about the client's expectations and vision for AI. Understanding what the customer wants to achieve using AI is critical for matching the technology with their strategic goals. Questions such as "What does success look like for you with AI in the next two to three years?" or "How do you envision AI transforming your business operations?" might assist the customer define their long-term objectives. This method also lays the groundwork for moderating expectations, particularly in circumstances where the client's understanding of AI is too optimistic or mismatched with existing technical capabilities.

Active listening is essential during the interview process. This entails not just hearing the client's remarks, but also responding with them in a way that indicates comprehension and stimulates more conversation. For example, summarizing their remarks or asking follow-up questions based on what they've said might demonstrate your genuine interest in understanding their requirements. This method fosters confidence and guarantees that the interview is a team effort rather than a one-sided interrogation.

Generally, conducting stakeholder interviews is an effective strategy for broadening the area of understanding. Often, many individuals inside a company will have differing viewpoints on how AI may help their operations. Interviewing stakeholders from multiple departments (such as marketing, finance, operations, and IT) offers a comprehensive understanding of the client's requirements. For example, the marketing team may be interested in AI-driven consumer segmentation, but the IT department may be focused on increasing cybersecurity using AI techniques. Collecting these different insights ensures that the AI solution targets all aspects of the company, resulting in more comprehensive and profitable outcomes.

8.3.Managing Client Expectations

Managing client expectations is an important part of delivering effective AI initiatives. Setting realistic objectives and timetables while controlling project scope ensures that the customer and the AI consultant are on the same page from the start, decreasing the possibility of misunderstandings or disappointments later in the process. In AI consulting, where projects frequently entail sophisticated algorithms, unanticipated data difficulties, and emerging technology, it is critical to create clear expectations to enable successful project execution.

Setting realistic goals is an important first step in managing client expectations. Many clients may have lofty expectations of what AI can do, which are frequently influenced by media hype or misunderstandings about AI's potential. As a consultant, it is critical to lead the client toward attainable goals that are consistent with both their business demands and the present level of AI technology. This necessitates an honest evaluation of what AI can and cannot achieve, particularly in light of the client's existing data and resources. For example, if a client expects to totally automate a complicated decision-making process, it is critical to highlight AI's limitations and where human oversight may still be required. Setting defined, incremental goals—such as using AI for certain activities before expanding to larger applications—can help manage expectations and create a road map for success.

Setting realistic timescales is another important aspect of expectation management. AI projects frequently need an ongoing process of testing, model training, and refining, which might take longer than customers expect. During the project planning phase, it is critical to give customers with a thorough understanding of the many steps involved in producing AI solutions, such as data collection and preparation, model construction, testing, and implementation

Breaking the project down into segments with clear deliverables at each level can help keep the customer involved and informed of progress. For example, indicating that data preparation may take weeks before model development can begin will help avoid misunderstandings later on when project schedules exceed the client's initial expectations. Setting milestones with precise dates may also assist in managing timelines by ensuring that the consultant and client are on the same page.

Managing project scope is another critical component of expectation management. Clients may initially seek a wide variety of AI functions, but as the project proceeds, it is sometimes discovered that particular features or objectives are more complicated than expected. Scope creep—when a project goes beyond its initial goals—can cause delays, financial overruns, and missed expectations. To avoid this, the project's scope should be defined early on and explicitly documented in the project plan. Any modifications to the scope should be reviewed and agreed upon prior to implementation, with an awareness of the impact on deadlines and costs. For example, if a customer requests new features mid-project, stating the additional time and resources necessary might help manage their expectations and keep the project on track.

Effective communication throughout the project is vital for managing expectations. Regular updates and progress reports keep the customer informed of any issues, changes, or delays that may occur during the project. Transparency in communication fosters trust and enables collaborative problem-solving when challenges arise. For example, if a machine learning model is not producing the expected results owing to data quality difficulties, openly communicating these challenges with the customer helps them to alter their expectations and better understand the reasons for any delays. Furthermore, conveying technical topics in understandable language guarantees that non-technical stakeholders can follow along and stay involved with the project's development.

Lastly, it is critical to establish quantifiable success criteria from the beginning of the project. Defining key performance indicators (KPIs) or metrics that will determine the project's success allows all parties to agree on what constitutes a good conclusion. Whether it's attaining a given degree of accuracy in a predictive model, lowering operational expenses by a certain percentage, or boosting customer engagement measures, having defined, quantifiable goals provide the project a real conclusion. This not only helps to control expectations, but it also gives a framework for assessing the project's performance when it is finished.

Ultimately, managing client expectations necessitates a mix of clear communication, thorough planning, and defining achievable objectives and timetables. AI consultants can keep their customers informed, involved, and happy with the end result by establishing the project scope early on, breaking down difficult activities into manageable parts, and keeping open discussion throughout the process. This method not only ensures project success, but it also develops long-term trust and great client relationships.

8.4.AI Proof of Concept (PoC) Development

Developing an AI Proof of Concept (PoC) is an important step in assessing if an artificial intelligence project is technically and commercially viable before spending heavily in its execution. A proof-of-concept (PoC) establishes the viability of an AI solution on a smaller, controlled scale, allowing enterprises to test assumptions, validate technology, and collect early feedback. Before moving forward with a full-scale implementation, a successful AI PoC may decrease risks, save time and costs, and instill trust in the AI solution.

1. Set clear objectives and success metrics.

The first step in developing a successful AI PoC is to establish clear objectives. This includes defining the precise business challenge that AI can solve and establishing the goals of the proof of concept. For example, if a corporation is looking into AI to automate customer care, the goal may be to create a chatbot capable of handling 50% of client concerns autonomously. Success metrics are critical for determining the efficacy of the PoC. Accuracy, reaction time, cost savings, and customer satisfaction are all examples of quantifiable metrics. A well-defined purpose and success criteria guarantee that the PoC aligns with corporate objectives and produces quantifiable results.

2. Select the Right Use Case.

Selecting the appropriate use case is critical to the success of an AI PoC. The chosen use case should have a clear business benefit and be an issue that AI can tackle effectively. It is critical to select a use case that is small enough to be controllable yet substantial enough to showcase the AI solution's capabilities. For example, a healthcare practitioner may try AI to improve diagnosis accuracy in detecting certain illnesses, such as lung cancer, using medical imaging. A well-defined use case helps to focus the proof of concept on achieving useful outcomes while avoiding excessive complexity.

3. Form a Cross-functional Team

An AI proof-of-concept involves collaboration across many teams, including data scientists, AI engineers, and domain specialists. The technical components of AI are handled by data scientists and engineers, who create the model, train it on data, and assess its performance. Domain expertise verify that the AI solution meets real-world business requirements and offers insights into unique industry difficulties. This partnership guarantees that the AI model not only works technically but also adds value for businesses. A cross-functional team with diversified experience is capable of efficiently addressing technical, operational, and strategic difficulties.

4. Prepare the dataset and tools.

A successful AI PoC is dependent on the availability of high-quality, representative data. Before beginning the PoC, it is critical to collect a clean, well-labeled dataset that will be used to train and test the AI model. The dataset should represent the real-world circumstances that the AI solution would experience, ensuring that the proof-of-concept results are meaningful and practical. Furthermore, picking the appropriate tools and frameworks is critical. TensorFlow, PyTorch, and cloud services such as AWS or Google Cloud provide the infrastructure required for rapid development and deployment of AI models. The tools used should be appropriate for the complexity of the use case and the team's technical skills.

5. Test and iterate the model.

Once the AI model has been created, it should be thoroughly evaluated on the provided dataset. The PoC phase enables the team to detect any flaws in the model, such as errors or biases, and make changes to enhance performance. The iterative process of testing and fine-tuning is critical for ensuring that the AI model fulfills success criteria. For example, a corporation evaluating an AI-driven recommendation system may realize that the original model is not making meaningful recommendations for specific consumer categories. By fine-tuning the model and integrating new data, the team may improve its accuracy and relevance.

6. *Evaluate and present results.*

After testing and improving the AI model, the next step is to compare the PoC outcomes to the established success criteria. If the PoC meets or surpasses expectations, it provides solid proof that the AI solution is ready for full-scale implementation. The study should involve a thorough examination of performance measures, financial ramifications, and possible business value. Presenting these results to stakeholders is crucial for getting support. It's critical to highlight both technological viability and commercial advantages, such as increased efficiency, cost reductions, or better customer experiences. A clear and data-driven presentation of findings increases confidence in moving forward with the AI solution.

However, A successful AI PoC involves careful preparation, a well-defined scope, cross-team collaboration, and iterative testing. Organizations may successfully analyze the viability of an AI project by following four steps: setting clear objectives, picking the appropriate use case, generating a high-quality dataset, and reviewing outcomes. A well-executed AI PoC lowers the risks associated with AI adoption, delivers useful insights, and builds the groundwork for successful full-scale deployment.

8.5. Client Communication and Reporting

Effective client communication and reporting are critical for ensuring transparency and confidence throughout the project's lifespan. Clear communication from the start ensures that all stakeholders are on the same page about goals, timetables, and expectations. A well-defined communication strategy should be created from the start, describing how and when updates will be delivered, what formats will be utilized, and who the major points of contact are. Regular communication allows you to address problems proactively, preventing misunderstandings or delays that might derail the project.

One of the most effective tactics is to provide regular status updates. These updates, whether in the form of emails, phone calls, or meetings, should include a brief review of project status, including completed milestones, ongoing work, impending targets, and any hazards. One aspect to good reporting is to convey information that is relevant to the client's perspective, concentrating on outcomes, timetables, and any influence on the client's company. Reports should also include graphics such as charts or graphs to make the information easier to understand, especially when working with complicated data.

In addition to planned updates, keeping an open channel of contact for ad hoc questions or unexpected situations is critical. When difficulties develop, prompt reporting and solution-oriented communication reassures the customer that their project is being managed appropriately. This builds trust and confidence. It is also critical to manage expectations by being honest about timetables and probable obstacles, so that the customer is not startled by delays or adjustments.

However, project wrap-up reporting should emphasize project accomplishments, difficulties addressed, and lessons gained. This last letter not only gives closure, but it also acts as a helpful reference for future projects, therefore strengthening the client connection and opening the path for possible repeat business.

Chapter Nine

Marketing and Growing Your AI Consulting Business

9.1. Introduction

Marketing and growing an AI consulting firm requires a deliberate approach that combines technical competence with effective communication and outreach. As AI technologies grow more popular across sectors, it is critical for AI consultants to differentiate themselves and demonstrate the value they can provide to potential customers. Positioning oneself as a thought leader, cultivating strong connections, and utilizing digital technologies to broaden your reach and exposure are all critical components of successful marketing in this field.

Identifying your specialization is one of the first stages in marketing an AI consulting company. Artificial Intelligence (AI) is a vast area with applications spanning from automation and predictive analytics to computer vision and natural language processing. You may establish yourself as an authority in addressing unique business difficulties by concentrating on particular sectors or specialized AI applications. You may customize your services and marketing initiatives to the particular requirements of that business, for example, by focusing on the healthcare, banking, or retail sectors. Emphasizing case studies, accomplished projects, or pertinent experience in your selected field may help draw in customers who are seeking for specific information and tested fixes.

Growing a firm that provides AI consulting services requires content marketing. You may become known as a thought leader by releasing blogs, whitepapers, and case studies that discuss the newest developments and difficulties in artificial intelligence. These papers should not only showcase your technical proficiency but also offer company executives practical advice on how AI might solve particular problems. To attract potential clients, consider creating a whitepaper about how artificial intelligence (AI) may improve supply chain management or lower customer attrition in a certain sector. You may also increase your reputation and exposure in the industry by giving talks at conferences, taking part in webinars, or having your voice heard on podcasts about AI and business transformation.

Another crucial element of marketing an AI consulting company is creating a powerful web presence. The cornerstone of your digital marketing initiatives should be a polished website that concisely describes your offerings, areas of specialization, and customer success stories. Search engine optimization (SEO) is necessary for your website to make sure that prospective customers can discover you while looking for AI consultancy services. Building trust with prospects who are investigating your skills may be facilitated by including client testimonials and exhibiting your work through case studies or portfolio items. Apart from your website, having an active presence on social networking sites such as LinkedIn and Twitter enables you to interact with industry trends, exchange ideas, and establish connections with possible partners and clients.

Networking and developing relationships are critical for expanding an AI consulting firm, particularly when it comes to securing long-term contracts or large-scale projects. Participating at industry events, both in person and virtually, can help you meet decision-makers interested in using AI solutions. Joining AI-related associations, attending conferences, and participating in AI-related forums or discussion groups might help you expand your professional network and offer up new business chances. Relationship-building also includes collaborations with other service providers or technology businesses, which can lead to referrals or joint ventures that broaden your reach.

Using digital advertising can help increase the exposure of your AI consulting company. By targeting certain sectors, job categories, or geographical areas with paid advertising on sites like LinkedIn or Google Ads, you can make sure the proper people see your message. LinkedIn advertisements aimed at CTOs and decision-makers in sectors like banking or healthcare, for example, may prompt questions from companies actively considering AI implementation. Retargeting advertising to people who have already visited your website can assist ensure that potential customers remember you when they weigh their alternatives.

Also, one of the most effective strategies for expanding any consulting firm, including AI, is word-of-mouth marketing. Clients that are happy with your AI solutions and have seen success with them are inclined to refer you to others. New business prospects can arise from promoting referrals through incentives, following up with clients for testimonials, and preserving great connections even after projects are over. Building a solid reputation for providing innovative, high-performing AI solutions is essential to expanding your clientele naturally through recommendations and favorable evaluations.

9.2. Building a Personal Brand as an AI Consultant

As an AI consultant, developing your own brand is crucial to gaining recognition, reaching a wider audience, and standing out in a crowded field. In an industry as specialized and fast changing as artificial intelligence, having a clear personal brand may assist draw in new customers, partnerships, and prospects. Your knowledge, distinctive selling point, and thought leadership in the AI field are all communicated through a powerful personal brand. Using social media channels, giving speeches, and creating material for blogs are important strategies for developing this brand.

Blogging is one of the best strategies for developing a personal brand. Providing intelligent, well-written information about the latest developments, problems, and trends in AI helps establish you as a thought leader. A well-written blog shows off your knowledge and offers your audience—whether they be other AI specialists, company executives, or prospective customers—useful information. When selecting blog themes, think about covering subjects related to the industry, new technology, or case studies that demonstrate the application of AI to practical issues. Write about the ethical implications of AI in healthcare, for instance, or how AI affects the shopping experience to draw in readers who are eager to learn from your experience. Furthermore, guest writing for prominent industry journals may help you expand your reach and establish yourself as a trusted authority in the AI sector.

Speaking engagements are another effective strategy for building your own brand as an AI expert. Participating in conferences, webinars, and panel discussions provides an opportunity to share your knowledge and interact with a larger audience. Speaking engagements give vital exposure and help you grow your reputation as an expert, whether you're explaining AI's technical features, providing ideas on its commercial applications, or researching industry trends. To get started, look for possibilities at AI-related events, technology conferences, and corporate innovation forums. As your credibility grows, you may be invited to more renowned events or requested to contribute to keynotes. Preparing extensively for these events—by supporting your thoughts with facts, sharing case studies, and providing practical takeaways—will help to develop your personal brand.

Social media is a vital tool for promoting your own brand, particularly in the AI consulting industry. LinkedIn, Twitter, and even YouTube enable you to demonstrate your knowledge, interact with your audience, and establish a community of followers. LinkedIn, in particular, is great for AI consultants since it provides a professional network where they can exchange papers, participate in industry discussions, and connect with future customers and colleagues. Regularly providing information, such as insights into AI advances, sharing blog entries, or commenting on important news, helps you keep exposure and promote yourself as a thought leader. Twitter allows you to join in topical AI topics by utilizing relevant hashtags, providing brief ideas, and connecting with other AI thought leaders. Hosting live Q&A sessions or seminars on platforms such as YouTube or LinkedIn Live allows you to directly communicate with your audience, resulting in deeper relationships and trust.

Consistency in messaging and appearance is also an important aspect of developing a personal brand. Consistency in everything you do, from the material you create to how you portray yourself online and in person, is critical to ensure that your audience knows your values. Your brand should reflect your distinct viewpoint on AI and approach to using technology to solve business challenges. Whether you specialize in AI ethics, machine learning for business transformation, or AI's influence on a certain sector, remaining consistent in your area of expertise helps you develop a clear and identifiable brand. Aligning your social media accounts, blog posts, and public speaking subjects with this brand strengthens your standing as an authority in your chosen field.

Ultimately, collaborating with other thought leaders or industry influencers might help you increase brand awareness. Co-authoring articles, engaging in collaborative webinars, or appearing as a guest on AI-focused podcasts will help you reach new audiences and boost your authority. Collaborating with influencers or established specialists in related industries, such as data science or digital transformation, may help you get cross-industry awareness, increase your reach, and strengthen your brand.

9.3. Networking and Partnerships

Networking and creating relationships are critical for success as an AI consultant because they allow you to connect with customers, cooperate with tech communities, and interact with industry leaders. Building a strong network not only opens up new business prospects, but it also gives access to insights, resources, and partnerships that may help you improve your expertise and reputation. In the rapidly changing AI world, cultivating relationships with the appropriate individuals helps that you keep ahead of industry trends while also opening doors to future collaborations and initiatives.

Building relationships with clients is a critical component of effective networking. While providing high-quality AI solutions is critical, building solid, long-term customer connections is also crucial. It begins with clear and regular communication in which you actively listen to their issues and ambitions. Following up with clients after a project is completed to give assistance, updates, or extra services can help to maintain a positive connection. Furthermore, delighted consumers are frequently your finest champions, recommending your services to others in their network. By demonstrating real interest in their business and providing value beyond the first contract, you may convert clients into long-term partners and potential referral sources.

Engaging with tech groups is another critical component of developing a strong network. Participating in AI-related forums, attending meetups, and joining online platforms such as GitHub or Reddit, where AI specialists share ideas, allows you to remain up to date on the newest advances in AI technology. These communities provide opportunities to work on open-source projects, discuss research findings, and seek advice from peers. By participating in conversations or providing answers to common problems, you establish yourself as a competent and helpful member of the community. This involvement can lead to significant partnerships with other individuals or firms, increasing your exposure and reputation in the AI area.

Building contacts with industry leaders is critical for further expanding your network. When industry influencers, such as AI thought leaders, researchers, or renowned corporate executives, promote or cooperate with you, you can get vital visibility and credibility. Attending industry conferences, webinars, or seminars in which influencers speak or participate is one method to interact with them. Introducing yourself and starting meaningful discussions with these people might put you on their radar. Furthermore, sharing their information on social media, commenting on their postings, or thoughtfully engaging to their debates might help to establish rapport. Over time, this can lead to chances for partnerships, joint ventures, and even public endorsements, which can raise your reputation.

Partnering with other technology companies is another effective networking method. AI consulting frequently crosses with other technologies, such as cloud computing, cybersecurity, or data science, creating potential for cooperation. Partnering with companies who specialize in complementary services allows you to provide more complete solutions to your clients. For example, collaborating with a data analytics firm might allow you to use their experience to provide a more integrated AI solution. Such collaborations not only broaden the breadth of services you may offer, but also allow you to tap into each other's customer networks, offering reciprocal prospects for development.

Active participation in business events and conferences is another effective way to expand your network. These events give an opportunity to meet experts from various industries who are interested in AI. Attending industry-specific conferences, such as those focusing on healthcare, finance, or manufacturing, allows you to network with decision-makers and business executives who are looking at AI solutions for their companies. Presenting at these events increases your visibility and helps you to demonstrate your knowledge. Following up with the people you met at conferences, whether via LinkedIn or email, ensures that you preserve those contacts and may transform them into significant professional ties.

Using social media sites such as YouTube, Twitter, and LinkedIn may also be a big help in growing your network. For instance, LinkedIn is a great resource for making connections with experts in many fields. Peers and potential clients alike might take notice when you share AI-related ideas, articles, or case studies. By mindfully like, sharing, and commenting on other people's work, you may interact with industry leaders and possible partners, expand your online visibility, and start conversations. On the other hand, Twitter may be used to follow industry influencers, stay up to date on AI news, and take part in conversations during events relevant to the sector. By consistently participating on these sites, you establish yourself as a knowledgeable and involved part of the AI and tech communities.

9.4. Creating a Consulting Portfolio

Developing a consulting portfolio is an effective method to demonstrate your skills, experience, and the value you provide to customers as an AI consultant. A well-organized portfolio showcases your previous work, case studies, and client testimonials, giving prospective clients real evidence of your expertise. This fosters trust and credibility by allowing potential clients to see how you can address their individual difficulties. An excellent portfolio is more than just a marketing tool; it also shows your particular expertise in delivering AI solutions.

A solid consulting portfolio starts with case studies that highlight your most significant initiatives. Every case study should include an overview of the client's issue, your suggested course of action, and the quantifiable outcomes that were attained. This story illustrates how you can use AI technology to solve practical business problems. For instance, your case study should include how you handled the data analysis, developed the model, and eventually enhanced inventory control or boosted sales if you assisted a retail organization in implementing AI-driven demand forecasting. To assist prospective clients realize your breadth of technical knowledge, be precise about the technology you employed, such as natural language processing or machine learning techniques. Case studies that are succinct and demonstrate successful results help clients have more faith in your capacity to deliver results for their own projects.

Incorporating a range of previous work within your portfolio is also vital. Highlighting projects from other sectors or AI applications demonstrates your versatility and adaptability. If you've worked on projects spanning from predictive analytics for a healthcare provider to chatbot creation for a financial services company, including these examples to illustrate your wide knowledge and ability to solve challenges across industries. Potential clients from various sectors will have more faith in your capacity to adjust AI solutions to their unique requirements if they see proof of successful outcomes in related domains. Furthermore, presenting projects at various degrees of complexity helps you to reach a broader spectrum of organizations, from startups searching for basic automation to corporations looking for more powerful AI systems.

Client testimonials are another important aspect of a consulting portfolio. Positive feedback from pleased clients acts as social proof, giving potential clients trust in your work. Testimonials may provide a personal touch by describing what it's like to work with you, your communication skills, and your dedication to achieving outcomes. When soliciting testimonials from clients, urge them to focus on specific parts of your service that struck out, such as your problem-solving ability, technical competence, or how your AI solution benefited their business processes. These testimonies are particularly powerful when accompanied by the client's name, title, and corporate logo, which lends legitimacy to the endorsement.

Your portfolio should also have graphic aspects that make it interesting and simple to explore. Incorporating charts, graphs, or before-and-after comparisons into your case studies may clearly demonstrate the impact of your work. A graph that shows how a machine learning model lowered error rates in predictions or improved efficiency over time, for example, is a clear, visual indication of progress. Screenshots of dashboards or AI tools you've created can help to improve your portfolio by offering them a look into the real goods and solutions you provide. Organizing your portfolio into categories based on sectors, project types, or AI applications will help potential clients rapidly identify samples that meet their requirements.

Another useful addition to your consulting portfolio is a description of the services and abilities you provide, along with real-world examples from previous projects. While case studies concentrate on end-to-end solutions, a services section enables you to showcase certain areas of expertise, such as natural language processing, computer vision, or AI ethical advice. Pairing each service with a brief overview of how you used it in a past project helps prospective clients see how these talents transfer into real-world results. This is especially valuable for clients who are still investigating AI options and may not yet have a clear picture of the specific solution they want.

However, keeping an up-to-date portfolio is critical for remaining relevant in the fast-evolving AI environment. As you finish new projects, be sure to update your portfolio with additional case studies and customer testimonials that showcase your most recent work. This guarantees that your portfolio always showcases your most relevant talents and accomplishments to prospective clients. Furthermore, as AI technologies advance, you can update your portfolio to emphasize your knowledge of cutting-edge tools and approaches, establishing yourself as an expert who remains at the forefront of AI innovation.

9.5. Pricing and Structuring Your Consulting Services

Pricing and organizing your consulting services is an important part of building a successful AI consulting firm. The way you price your services and arrange contracts may have an influence on both profitability and the duration of customer relationships. As an AI consultant, you must create a price model that reflects the value of your knowledge, is competitive in the market, and fits within your customers' budget. Furthermore, designing contracts to encourage long-term engagements ensures stability and the opportunity for deeper collaborations with customers.

When it comes to pricing your services, you have various options. One frequent technique is hourly or daily charges, which are appropriate for short-term projects or clients that want flexibility. However, relying only on time might occasionally underestimate the strategic and technical knowledge you bring to the table. To decide a reasonable hourly or daily charge, evaluate your degree of skill, the complexity of the activity, and current AI consulting industry prices. Senior AI consultants, for example, might charge greater prices because of their specific understanding. Conducting market research to evaluate your rates against rivals can assist you guarantee you remain competitive while earning what you deserve are worth.

Alternatively, many consultants prefer project-based pricing, which involves charging a set price for producing a certain outcome or completing a defined scope of work. This strategy may appeal to clients since it gives them a clear idea of prices up front and allows you to price your services based on the value you generate rather than the time spent. For example, if you're creating a custom AI solution that dramatically enhances a client's operational efficiency, your pricing should match its commercial value.

Project-based pricing might also encourage you to work effectively because you will be paid for the results rather than the hours worked. However, it is critical to explicitly define the project's scope in order to minimize scope creep, which occurs when more work beyond the initial agreement is required without additional remuneration. Retainer-based pricing is a common approach for long-term partnerships. In this agreement, the customer pays a set sum per month or quarter for continuous advisory services. This is especially beneficial for clients that want ongoing assistance, such as organizations who require frequent AI system maintenance, upgrades, or strategic counsel. Retainers provide stability for both the consultant and the client—clients have constant access to your knowledge, and you benefit from a consistent pay stream. Retainer agreements often involve a certain number of hours or deliverables per month and can be tailored to cover both strategic advice services and hands-on AI development work. Structure retainers with a tiered pricing model, allowing customers to select different levels of assistance based on their needs, may make your services more flexible and accessible to businesses of all kinds.

Another important part of pricing is deciding how much to charge for new services or changes in scope. In AI consulting, it is not commonplace for a project to change as the client acquires a better grasp of AI's capabilities or as new issues occur. Having a clear process for dealing with scope modifications is critical to safeguarding your time and ensuring you are adequately rewarded for any additional work. One solution is to include a condition in your contract that sets an hourly rate or extra price for work that falls outside the scope of the original assignment. This transparency guarantees that you and your customer are on the same page from the start, reducing misunderstandings as the project continues.

When creating consulting contracts, it is critical to explicitly define the scope of work, deliverables, dates, and payment conditions. The contract should clearly state what the customer may anticipate from you, whether it is a fully installed AI system, a strategic AI roadmap, or a series of workshops. Consider breaking down bigger, more complex projects into phases or milestones, with remuneration attached to the accomplishment of each stage. This not only gives clients peace of mind, but also assures that you get paid as the project proceeds. Milestone-based contracts also allow for alterations at critical stages of the project if the scope changes or new requirements arise.

Contracts should also cover intellectual property (IP) rights and ownership of the AI models, algorithms, or solutions that you develop. Clients often expect to own the solutions you produce, but in some situations, you may want to maintain control of specific unique technology or tools. To avoid future problems, it is critical to explain these words ahead of time. Furthermore, if you're working on extremely sensitive or secret projects, incorporating non-disclosure agreements (NDAs) within the contract can assist in securing both your intellectual property and the client's data.

Lastly, designing your services around long-term engagements can lead to more meaningful customer connections. Instead of focusing on one-time initiatives, present yourself as a strategic partner that can guide customers through their AI journey over time. This might include providing continuous support after an AI installation, such as monitoring system performance, updating software, or providing extra training to the client's personnel. Regular check-ins, follow-up meetings, and delivering updates or new AI capabilities may all indicate your dedication to the client's success, increasing the chances of long-term partnership.

However, pricing and organizing your consulting services necessitate careful evaluation of your skills, the value you provide, and your clients' requirements. Whether using hourly rates, project-based fees, or retainers, your pricing strategy should account for both the intricacy of the task and the commercial effect of your AI solutions. Contracts with explicit terms on scope, milestones, and intellectual property rights facilitate seamless engagements and build long-term client relationships that benefit both sides.

References

1. Chatterjee , R., (2020). Fundamental concepts of artificial intelligence and its applications, Journal of Mathematical Problems, Equations and Statistics, ; 1(2): 13-24.
2. Singh, A. and Noida, Y. E. and Pradesh, U. *2019). The Concept of Artificial Intelligence Journal of Emerging Technologies and Innovative Research, Volume 6, Issue 3, pp. 566-570.
3. Goodfellow, I., Bengio, Y., & Courville, A. (2016). Deep learning. MIT Press.
4. Russell, S., & Norvig, P. R. (2021). ARTIFICIAL INTELLIGENCE: A Modern Approach, Global Edition.
5. Rahımova, G. E., (2024). Development trends of the concept of Artificial intelligence, E3S Web of Conferences 538, 02021, https://doi.org/10.1051/e3sconf/202453802021
6. Mishra, S., Clark, J., Perrault, C.R. (2020). Measurement in AI Policy: Opportunities and Challenges. http://arxiv.org/abs/2009.09071 15.
7. Perry, B., Uuk, R. (2019). Big Data and Cognitive Computing, 3(2), 1–17. https://doi.org/10.3390/bdcc3020026.
8. Phillips-Wren, G. (2012). AI Tools In Decision Making Support Systems: A Review. Journal of Emerging Technologies in Accounting, https://doi.org/10.2308/jeta-19-04- 30-21
9. Sartori, L., Bocca, G. (2022). AI and Society, 38(2), 443–458. https://doi.org/10.1007/s00146-022-01422-1
10. Sinha, S., Lee, Y.M. (2024). Challenges with developing and deploying AI models and applications in industrial systems. *Discov Artif Intell* **4**, 55, https://doi.org/10.1007/s44163-024-00151-2
11. Garcia, E., & Martinez, L. (2023). Integrating AI capabilities into consulting service offerings. Journal of Professional Services Marketing, 39(2), 178-193.
12. Garcia, E., & Martinez, L. (2024). Client education strategies for AI-enhanced consulting services. Journal of Consulting Practice, 28(3), 312-327.
13. Garcia, E., & Smith, T. (2023). The rise of AI-facilitated crowdsourced consulting platforms. Gig Economy Journal, 7(4), 423-438.
14. Garcia, J., Brown, A., & Lee, S. (2024). Mitigating algorithmic bias in AI-powered consulting tools. AI Ethics Journal, 5(2), 89-104.
15. Johnson, A., & Lee, S. (2023). Data privacy challenges in AI-driven consulting practices. Journal of Business Ethics, 174(3), 567-582.
16. Johnson, A., & Lee, S. (2024). AI-enhanced knowledge sharing in consulting: Implications and opportunities. Knowledge Management Research & Practice, 22(1), 45-60.

17. Johnson, E., Lee, S., & Brown, A. (2024). Pricing strategies for AI-augmented consulting services. Journal of Revenue and Pricing Management, 23(2), 178-193.
18. Thompson, J., & Lee, S. (2023). AI-powered competitive intelligence in strategic consulting. Competitive Intelligence Review, 34(2), 178-193.
19. Kaif, K. M., Singh, R., and Vedan, J., (2024). Artificial Intelligence (AI) A Boon for Marketing, Journal of Advanced Research in Service Management Volume 7, Issue 1, pp. 32-53.
20. Haleem, A., Javaid, M., Qadri, M. A., Singh, R. P., & Suman, R. (2022). "Artificial intelligence (AI) applications for marketing: A literature-based study." International Journal of Intelligent Networks, Vol 3, pp. 119-132.
21. Reddy, K. V., Sreenivas, T., & Lavanya, G. (2023). " AI marketing: How to use artificial intelligence for cause-related marketing. AIP Conference Proceedings, Vol 2821, No 1.
22. Vlačić, B., Corbo, L., Costa e Silva, S., & Dabić, M. (2021). "The Evolving Role of Artificial Intelligence in Marketing: A Review and Research Agenda." Journal of Business Research, Vol 128, pp. 187-203

www.ingramcontent.com/pod-product-compliance
Lightning Source LLC
LaVergne TN
LVHW081530050326
832903LV00025B/1717